WHAT IS YOUR I.Q. (ICE QUOTIENT)?

Test it with these questions:

- Which great scorer became a hero by not scoring?

- Who are the members of the Detroit Red Wings who embarrassed Punch Imlach?

- Can you name the "Mod-Man" of the National Hockey League?

- Is Bobby Orr really that good?

- Will Buffalo and Vancouver succeed as big-league cities?

You may not be in the "hockey genius" category yet, but you will be after finding the answers to these and other questions in

HOCKEY STARS OF 1971

STAN FISCHLER, author of a syndicated column, "Inside Hockey," has written numerous books including *Gordie Howe, Goal!, Stan Mikita, The Turbulent Career of a Hockey Superstar, Hockey!*, and *Bobby Orr and the Big, Bad Bruins*. He lives with his wife, Shirley, pet puli, Chazy, and pet cat, Sybil in New York City. He expects Mrs. Fischler to become the first female hockey writer so that he may retire and become a Maple Leaf fan again.

HOCKEY STARS
OF 1971

STAN FISCHLER

Research Assistant JORY LEVINTON

PYRAMID BOOKS • NEW YORK

To Toots, Who Helps Keep Me Onside

HOCKEY STARS OF 1971

A PYRAMID BOOK

First printing, November 1970

Copyright © 1970 by Stan Fischler

All Rights Reserved

Printed in the United States of America

PYRAMID BOOKS are published by Pyramid Publications
A Division of The Walter Reade Organization, Inc.
444 Madison Avenue, New York, New York 10022, U.S.A.

TABLE OF CONTENTS

THE SEASON PAST

A chance, off-the-cuff remark by an obscure member of the Chicago Black Hawks mushroomed into the most decisive factor in 1969-70, the most bizarre season in National Hockey League history.

Before the start of the campaign, little Pit Martin of Chicago denounced the majority of his colleagues as selfish and lacking teamwork. By implication, he indicted stars such as Bobby Hull and Stan Mikita for receiving preferential treatment and asserted that only a complete change in the Black Hawks' philosophy could redeem the potentially strong team.

The change came and so did the redemption.

Bobby Hull became a holdout and missed the first 14 games of the season. Management eventually brought him to his knees and The Golden Jet returned both penitent and persuaded he would have to change his style. Which he did. Hockey's greatest contemporary goal-scorer became defense-oriented. Stan Mikita, the other half of Chicago's gold-dust twins also adjusted to the role of being "one of the boys".

Manager Tommy Ivan ordered the change and coach Billy Reay carried out the command. "We decided it would be all hockey for a change," said Reay, "with no outside distractions."

Seven months after Hull returned to the lineup the Chicago Black Hawks finished first in the East Division and won The Prince of Wales Trophy. It was an arresting upset.

In so doing, the Hawks wrought two stunning surprises —they caught and then edged the Boston Bruins who had held first-place late in the homestretch, and they helped oust the Montreal Canadiens from a playoff berth for the

7

first time in 22 years. And by finishing on top, the Black Hawks became the first NHL team ever to leap from the cellar to first place in one season.

Since both Montreal and Toronto finished fifth and sixth, respectively, it marked the first time the Stanley Cup playoffs were held without a Canadian entry.

What made all the events so unreal was the fact that none of the playoff positions were finally decided until the final day of the season; and, at that, some higher mathematics were involved to settle matters. Both Boston and Chicago completed the season with 99 points but the Hawks annexed first on the strength of having five more victories than the Bruins. Detroit's Red Wings, who had not made it to the playoffs in four years, wound up third. Then there were New York and Montreal tied in games won and lost. According to league rules, the team with the most goals would annex fourth and the Rangers did so in still another unexpected series of episodes.

The Rangers entered the final day of the season trailing Montreal by two points in the standings and five tallies in the goals-scored column. That meant, to make the playoffs, New York not only had to win and hope Montreal lost to Chicago to square the points and victories totals, but also had to score at least five more goals against Detroit than the Canadiens did against the Black Hawks.

New York blitzed Detroit 9-5 on the final Sunday afternoon whereupon the Black Hawks trounced Montreal, 10-2 in the evening of April 5, 1970. Both the Rangers and Canadiens lifted their goalies in the final minutes, ignoring empty net opposition goals in an effort to increase their own scoring totals. As pulsating as the finish was, it also was tainted with severe criticism on several counts.

The NHL office was chastised for relying on the system of settling key positions by the games-won and goals-scored system. It was demanded that a playoff be held between the tied teams. In addition, the idea of both New York and Montreal pulling their goaltenders so early in the game was considered farcical by many critics.

Even more damaging to hockey was the effort displayed by the Red Wings against the Rangers on Sunday afternoon. Detroit, instead of playing its top line of Gordie

Howe-Alex Delvecchio-Frank Mahovlich, opened the
game with a fourth-rate unit and immediately was
bombed by the Rangers. Denunciations of the Red Wings'
alleged lack of effort zeroed in on the Detroiters from all
areas of the continent. Manager Sid Abel of the Red
Wings countered that he felt obliged to rest his weary
aces; that his players tried their best and that the Rangers
were unstoppable. But so revered an observer as Dick
Young of the *New York Daily News* echoed the opinions
of the opposition when he replied: "You have a moral
responsibility to your league, to your sport and to your
conscience to put out 100 per cent as long as something is
at stake, as there was for the Rangers and to Montreal."

The tumultuous and somewhat cloudy finish failed to
obscure the brighter aspects of the season. By far the most
generous glow was provided by Bobby Orr, the young
blond Bruins' defenseman who scored 33 goals and 87
assists and became the first backliner ever to lead the
NHL in scoring. The result, obviously, was that Orr revolutionized the concept of defensive play so that it now has
become as *de rigueur* for a defenseman to be offense-
minded as it is to stay behind his blue line. In addition it
became perfectly fashionable to suggest that Orr is the
greatest player of all time, better than Gordie Howe, Jean
Beliveau and Eddie Shore.

"There's never been one like him," said Bruins coach
Harry Sinden, "and there will never be another. He's the
type of guy who could break the goal-scoring record. And
he also could become the finest defenseman the game has
ever known." Retirement did not alter Sinden's view.

Orr's lustre overshadowed the excellent season of his
teammate, Phil Esposito who finished second in scoring
with 99 points. Meanwhile in Chicago Phil's kid brother,
Tony, startled the NHL with a record-breaking 15
shutouts as the Black Hawks produced the best goals
against average (2.24) in the league.

Another surprise was Chicago's ability to incorporate
collegians Keith Magnuson and Cliff Koroll into the regular lineup. A lean, red-haired defenseman, Magnuson
emerged as a fiery leader and one of the better backliners
in the league.

The Black Hawks' climb to the top was agonizingly

slow. From December through the beginning of March the New York Rangers tenaciously held first place and appeared capable of going all the way. But in mid-February the New Yorkers encountered a crippling series of injuries to such regulars as Brad Park, Jim Neilson, Don Marshall and Vic Hadfield. New York slipped from the top to the second division.

Meanwhile, the Red Wings, fortified with Carl Brewer on defense and the surprisingly high-scoring of young center Garry Unger, remained a contender throughout the season and actually had a chance to finish first up until the last week of the campaign. For Detroit the most remarkable accomplishment was the ability of Gordie Howe to lead the team in scoring although he was, at 42, the oldest player in the league.

In Boston the sentiment was that Harry Sinden's Bruins would finish first if the Canadiens could be caught. This, however, was a belief held before veteran defenseman Ted Green suffered a fractured skull in a stick-swinging duel with Wayne Maki of St. Louis in a pre-season game. The injury sidelined Green for the season and forced Sinden to re-align his defense. It weakened the Bruins and lowered them to a competitive par with the Black Hawks and Red Wings. A healthy Green very likely would have led the Bruins to the Prince of Wales Trophy.

"Teddy reached his peak for us in the 1969 playoffs," said Bruins' manager Milt Schmidt. "Remembering that, I'd say his absence made at least ten points difference in the 1969-70 season."

The Bruins were manacled by other problems in the early part of the schedule. High-scoring Ken Hodge was sidelined by an emergency appendectomy; hard-checking Derek Sanderson was bothered by knee and hip ailments; and Ron Murphy, who played on the record-breaking Phil Esposito line, had to retire because of a back ailment. As the Bruins struggled along they became enveloped in a fog of dissension. After he returned to the lineup Hodge rebelled against coach Sinden for benching him before a mid-season game. The more defensive-minded Don Marcotte was elevated from Hershey and suddenly the Bruins caught fire.

Sanderson returned. Hodge reformed and Boston began

getting steady goaltending from Eddie Johnston and Gerry Cheevers. The Bruins climbed past Detroit, Chicago and New York into first place, apparently for good. But the Black Hawks kept in close pursuit and finally caught Boston after the Bruins lost a game to Montreal in the final week of the season. "No complaints from me," said Sinden. "We went into Montreal and the Canadiens bombed us. Chicago went in and bombed the Canadiens. They did what we didn't do."

If the Bruins' failure to finish first was a disappointment, the Canadiens' descent to fifth place was regarded as absolutely calamitous. Only a year earlier Montreal won both the Prince of Wales Trophy and the Stanley Cup. Now they were has-beens and the reasons were plentiful. Captain Jean Beliveau had aged to a point where he lost his old spark. He had been coaxed into playing another season—apparently against his will—and, for the most part, skated like a man who was pushed to do something that grated his conscience. On top of that the Canadiens were torn by dissension, much more than the Bruins.

Sophomore coach Claude Ruel was given a race horse by his players after the 1969 Stanley Cup victory; now they were giving him the Bronx cheer. By late February Ruel got the message and finally offered to quit. "If they don't play for me," he warned, "then they can get someone else for behind that bench. There is no way I'm going to get sick for them when they won't produce for me. Every game we have one bad period, make three or four stupid mistakes. Then they die on me, won't fight back. They think they can play it by ear, wait for the puck to come to them. You have to go after that puck. You only win by hard work."

The one Canadien who always delivered the hard work was John Ferguson. But the tough left winger suffered a series of injuries that sidelined him during key portions of the season. Ruel's offer to resign was studied by manager Sam Pollock and rejected. Pollock instead offered Ruel a new contract with a salary increase. Pollock was going to stick by his "boy" and chop players instead. He'd already cut Dick Duff and dealt him to Los Angeles. When goalie Gump Worsley refused to take a temporary demotion to the American League he was suspended and later dealt to Minnesota where he led the North Stars in a late-season surge into the playoffs.

Minus Worsley the Canadiens were compelled to rely on goalies Rogatien Vachon and rookie Phil Myre. The goaltending was mediocre to average. In the end Vachon wilted and the Canadiens slipped out of a playoff berth. Their Canadian compatriots, the Maple Leafs, also were burdened with injuries throughout the campaign and never received the big effort from high-priced Norm Ullman and Tim Horton. Rookie coach John McLellan nevertheless kept Toronto respectable for most of the season. The Leafs faded in the final month and can only look back on the play of captain Dave Keon and Ron Ellis with any degree of satisfaction.

Despite attempts by the NHL executives to glorify its West Division, the expansion section remained typically inferior to its East counterpart and almost consistently mediocre. The intersectional scoreboard betrayed the difference. Eastern teams won 133 games while western clubs just 41, and there were 42 ties. Significantly, games between the western sextets and Montreal and Toronto often had less than sellout crowds in Maple Leaf Gardens and The Forum. Normally these two Canadian arenas easily sell out for games against the East.

Once again Scotty Bowman's St. Louis Blues ran away with the Clarence Campbell Bowl, emblematic of supremacy in the West. For a change the Pittsburgh Penguins, who missed the playoffs for two straight years, made it this time under the studious direction of coach Red Kelly. Oakland's Seals, a team that appeared ready to fold several times during the campaign, lumbered into third place and the Minnesota North Stars somehow managed to squeeze into fourth past the favored Philadelphia Flyers. A study in despair, the Los Angeles Kings finished an abysmal last. Their only claim to newsworthiness was the trading of defensemen Bill White and Dale Rolfe to Chicago and Detroit, respectively. Both deals considerably aided the eastern teams and did little to bolster the Kings.

If the demise of the Los Angeles club accomplished anything it was to mute the decibel count of Kings' owner Jack Kent Cooke. It is doubtful if Los Angeles could duplicate its subterranean efforts again—the Kings' leading scorer, Ross Lonsberry, finished 44th on the NHL list.

Spectator counts as much as goal-scoring absorbed the interest of West Division-watchers. St. Louis, Minnesota and Philadelphia became proven box-office hits. Despite a competitive team, Pittsburgh continued to lag at the gate and Los Angeles suffered appropriately low attendance. The situation at Oakland was so grave that players worried about where their next paycheck would come from.

The NHL would cover any debts to the players but the question remained: was Oakland fit to be an NHL city? Certainly playoff attendance once again indicated it wasn't. The Penguin-Seal series drew flies in both rinks and a rumor circulated that the California club would be transferred to Long Island, N.Y., a report that later was dismissed by the league.

As expected, the West Division playoffs were relatively boring. Pittsburgh won from Oakland in four straight and St. Louis was extended to six games—a minor upset—by the North Stars. With Kelly behind the bench, the Penguins were thought capable of taming the Blues in the Western final. St. Louis easily captured the opening two games on home ice, both outscoring and outfighting the smaller Pittsburgh skaters. Then the series moved to Pittsburgh where the Penguins scored two hard-fought one-goal victories, but St. Louis took the next two games and entered the Stanley Cup final for the third year in a row.

For two consecutive years the Blues had been humiliated in the Cup finals by the Montreal Canadiens who beat them in eight straight games. This time, however, St. Louis was up against a new foe in the last round and there was reason to believe that Scotty Bowman's team would do better; especially since the Blues would be at home for the first two games.

But, once again, the East Division representative delivered a humiliating defeat to the Blues. They not only lost in four straight games to Boston but were easily manhandled on St. Louis ice. The series proved what most serious hockey observers had suspected all along—that the West Division was nothing more than a glorified minor league and the Blues had no more right to challenge for the

Stanley Cup than the Toronto Maple Leafs who finished last in the East Division.

The Blues also raised an interesting question—if they were the laughing stock of the playoffs, what fate would befall the inept new Buffalo Sabres and Vancouver Canucks in 1970-71? It was a question that was awesome and frightening and only time will tell how serious it would be.

So thundrous was the final week of the season in the East Division that the Stanley Cup playoffs were expected to be anti-climactic. But New York and Boston nurtured a bitter rivalry and the Chicago-Detroit series promised some histrionics.

The Bruins easily outplayed the Rangers in the first two games at Boston Garden but the Rangers rebounded in the next two at New York amid a succession of fights and wrestling matches. The teams set a Stanley Cup record of 375 penalty minutes for the six games as the Bruins prevailed with a comeback 3-2 win in the fifth game and a comfortable 4-1 sweep in the sixth. Meanwhile the Black Hawks brushed aside the Red Wings with surprising ease in four straight. The East Division final against the Bruins opened at Chicago Stadium.

Blessed with the home ice advantage the Hawks leaped to the attack but were blunted by acrobatic Gerry Cheevers in the Bruins' net. Suddenly the Boston sextet captured the momentum and pumped six goals past Tony Esposito for a 6-3 win. Two nights later the Bruin forwards—and Bobby Orr—toyed with the beleaguered Hawks and skated off with a 4-1 victory. It became obvious that Esposito was playing inferior hockey, but Chicago coach Billy Reay chose to stick with him rather than his excellent alternate, Gerry Desjardins. This proved to be a fatal mistake as the Bruins overwhelmed Esposito in the next two games at Boston and moved into the East-West final to rout St. Louis.

THE SEASON PRESENT

The addition of Buffalo and Vancouver to the National Hockey League increased representation from 12 to 14 teams and caused a major upheaval. Vancouver, the most geographically western of NHL teams, was placed in the East Division along with Buffalo. To achieve a numerical balance Chicago was transferred to the West Division and, irrational as the settings appeared, the NHL was ready for the 1970-71 season with the usual surplus of optimism.

There were two sources of enthusiasm. Bobby Orr of the Bruins had emerged as the brightest star of major league sports and both Buffalo and Vancouver were almost assured of huge profits in their first year of operation. And this despite some rather strange choices to run these teams.

The Canucks of Vancouver chose Norman "Bud" Poile as general manager, a selection which in and of itself underlines the curious logic behind hockey moves. Poile managed the Philadelphia Flyers when they joined the NHL. The Flyers finished first in their rookie year but then got progressively worse. Early in the 1969-70 season Flyer chairman Ed Snider fired Poile because of his displeasure over the club's performance. As a free agent Poile suddenly found himself invited to nurture the new Vancouver entry.

One of his first moves was to hire Hal Laycoe, who had been fired as Los Angeles coach about the same time that Poile had been deposed in Philadelphia. This was doubly astonishing since Poile and Laycoe had long been regarded as bitter enemies. "Laycoe was flabbergasted," said Poile. "We hadn't talked for 11 years. We had the kind of mutual admiration society that makes wars. Always, in the

15

past, I hired my best friends to work for me. Now I'm trying a new approach. I hired my best enemy on the grounds that he's a better hockey man than Jack Cooke (the L.A. owner) deserved."

Laycoe wasn't about to cut off his nose to spite his face. He told Poile, "I'll be on the next plane."

The Canucks then went about the business of selling tickets for their large and lavish arena. Hockey interest was so high that management decided to cut off the subscription sale at about 12,000. Sellouts were assured through April 1971.

Meanwhile the Buffalo Sabres also were hustling for a loser. They found one in George "Punch" Imlach, who had led the Toronto Maple Leafs out of a playoff berth in 1969. He was subsequently fired by President Stafford Smythe and was subsequently grabbed up by Seymour Knox, head of the new Buffalo sextet. Imlach was a contender for the Vancouver managership, but he decided to become both manager and coach of the Buffalo entry. "I've always believed that everything happens for the best," said Imlach. "I realize the Buffalo job is a tough one and that is the way I would rather have it. The terms and the conditions were so good that it was impossible for me to turn the job down. This is a job of building from the bottom. I've done it before and I can do it again."

The difference between Vancouver and Buffalo was that the Sabres entered the league owning just a handful of players whereas the Canucks purchased both the Rochester club of the American League and the old Vancouver Canucks of the Western League for a total of more than 50 skaters. Poile insisted that the figure was deceptive. "All the experts talked about the 55 players we owned in Vancouver and Rochester," he said. "That's nonsense. In that mob of minor leaguers we had 11 or 12 who retired, or who should retire."

While Vancouver and Buffalo chose to launch their NHL lives with somewhat jaded hockey leaders, the old-time Detroit Red Wings took a completely different—and somewhat enlightened—perspective. Realizing that more and more hockey players were coming from the university level, the Wings hired, for the first time, a college coach to run their bench.

Ned Harkness, a 48-year-old former Royal Canadian Air Force bombardier, is the man. For seven years Harkness coached at Cornell University and molded the Big Red into a dreadnought on ice. Last season Cornell put together a 29-0 record, including the NCAA championship, the best in the history of college hockey.

To obtain Harkness the Wings came up with a $50,000 contract and plenty of verbal persuasion. This was accomplished partially on the strength of Harkness' friendship with Red Wing manager Sid Abel, who ran the club from the bench in 1969-70. "Ned's approach will be different from mine," said Abel, "but I'm sure the players will accept it."

Prime acceptance was necessary from owner Bruce Norris. "Ned's record speaks for itself," said Norris. "We had talked over many choices and decided it would be best to pick an outsider. It was a new concept . . . actually we always wanted Ned, we just didn't know if we could get him."

One of the major questions confronting Harkness is just how veterans like Gordie Howe will react to the former college mentor. "I don't anticipate any problems," said Harkness. "I expect to learn a lot from Gordie. The name of the game is skating. I believe in discipline and conditioning. You can't win without them; there are no short cuts to success."

Howe vowed that this, his 25th year, will be his last. The Red Wings still revolve around Gordie and Harkness' success will in large part depend on Howe's durability. The Wings should be just good enough to gain a playoff berth, ahead of Buffalo, Vancouver and Toronto—because the Leafs, among other dilemmas, are still recuperating from the deals thoughtlessly made by Imlach two years ago.

"A major cause of the Leafs' trouble lies higher up," The Toronto Daily Star declared in a major editorial, "in a top management which (unlike Montreal's) has consistently appeared to put more emphasis on making money than on the style and quality of hockey it purveyed . . . Leaf fans have felt for years that the Maple Leaf Gardens management was squeezing them for every available cent; now, since they must now watch a poor team for their money, they are beginning to return the management's contempt."

Like the Maple Leafs, Montreal's Canadiens face the 1970-71 season with more than the normal amount of difficulties. They are no longer a championship club. They no longer reflect the confident management and long-standing savoir-faire that accompanies Stanley Cups. They must climb up rather than look down.

By contrast the New York Rangers, who helped dethrone the Canadiens last year, are in an excellent position to challenge the Boston Bruins and Chicago for the top. Armed with such enthusiastic young players as Brad Park, Jack Egers and Walt Tkaczuk, the New Yorkers have the nucleus of a contender. Their debit, chronically, has been the inability to cope with the hard-hitting brand of hockey generated by the Bruins. This marks the 31st year since the Rangers won the Stanley Cup and the 29th since they finished first. Their fans have become frustrated and disillusioned, and there are no indications that this state of affairs will be altered in 1971, primarily, because the Bruins are stronger.

On these pages last year I picked the Bruins to win The Stanley Cup and I expect them to do it again in 1971. The reasons are obvious. However, new Coach Tom Johnson may be too inexperienced for the NHL. The attack is the most awesome in the league and the goaltending is adequate. Knitting all this together is Bobby Orr, the most all-inclusive player hockey has known; the league's leading scorer, the league's leading defenseman and the game's most magnetic personality. There is no reason barring an inordinate number of injuries, overconfidence or the complete disablement of Orr, why Boston shouldn't romp through the East Division and the playoffs.

The West Division, which has been the joke of the NHL since its formation four years ago, has received an infusion of respectability this year with the addition of the Black Hawks. This, of course, means that the phony "reign" of the St. Louis Blues will be ended when the Hawks annex first place and the Clarence Campbell Bowl without too much difficulty.

Chicago boasts power from the goal to the front line. The defense, anchored by Bill White, Keith Magnuson,

Doug Jarrett and Pat Stapleton, is among the best in the league. Tony "Zero" Esposito and Gerry Desjardins give Chicago the best one-two goaltending support in hockey and up front there's power. If the Black Hawks can maintain the diligence that marked their play last year they should be as strong as any NHL club—with the possible exception of the Bruins.

Directed by Scotty Bowman, a clever hockey man, the Blues no doubt will skate into second place. They have some capable forwards in the likes of Red Berenson, and Frank St.Marseille, a reliable defense and solid goaltending. But St. Louis simply is not in Chicago's class, a fact which will be proven throughout the season.

After Chicago and St. Louis, the West Division has the usual hodgepodge of minor leaguers—with a few key exceptions—masquerading in big-league uniforms.

Choosing between the Penguins, North Stars, Seals and Kings is like buying a car and trying to differentiate between various shades of grey. Because of their absurd trades and inept leadership the Kings can be counted on to finish last. For virtually the same reason, only on a more modest scale, the North Stars will be just a cut ahead of Los Angeles. That leaves the Penguins and the Seals and, from this vantage point the Pittsburgh sextet appears a trifle stronger.

Balancing the quality players around the league remains a great problem for the NHL and it won't be solved this year or the next. Thus, we can expect top-heavy East and West Divisions in 1970-71. Only the inveterate optimists like Bobby Orr can envision a balanced, more competitive situation in the league.

"I'm sure in a few years the Western Division will be equal with the East," says Orr, "and the competition will be so much better."

Not if Bobby Orr is still playing for the Bruins.

RED BERENSON

When Red Berenson led the West Division of the NHL in scoring during the 1968-69 season it was considered a prime example of pan-flashing that could not be repeated.

It is history now that Berenson did not repeat only because teammate Phil Goyette came up with an extraordinary season. But there was Berenson right behind with 33 goals and 39 assists for 72 points, good enough to place him seventh in the scoring race and good enough to win praise from various league precincts—plus the assurance that he's not a flash in the pan.

"It's not just that Red gets the big goal," explained St. Louis manager-coach Scotty Bowman, "but that he makes good plays and checks and digs. How many other players in this game score 30 or 35 goals a season and play defense too?"

Not many, which explains why Berenson is the most valuable member of the Blues and, until the Black Hawks arrived this year, the most accomplished all-round player in the West Division. Considering the enfeebled quality of the expansion section until 1970, this is faint praise but Berenson has more than proven he is a competent center. And he remains in the record-book, having scored six goals against Philadelphia in November 1968.

"It's kind of hard living up to that game," says Berenson. "I just try to do the best I can all the time."

The St. Louis center is unique not merely for his hockey-playing. He is, quite simply, a fascinating character.

Mostly, you can see it in Red Berenson's eyes. They come at you with an aura of inquisitiveness, distilled with thoughtfulness and humor. They are a different pair of eyes of a different kind of hockey player. Of all the skaters in the National Hockey League nobody hears a more different drummer than Red Berenson.

The tall St. Louis Blues center could be passed off as some kind of a nut by people who think a man interested in Indian lore is 'way out. He could be dismissed as a wildman because he likes nothing better than camping in the North Woods among the grizzlies and the rattlers. He could be labeled as highbrow because he is a voracious reader with a keen intellectual appetite.

He is all this, which is why Berenson must be one of the—if not *THE*—most fascinating character in the NHL today. Of course his wife, Joy, doesn't hinder him a bit.

"Joy and I are interested in the outdoors," says Berenson. "We like being in the wilderness and experiencing the country as it was years ago; the sheer beauty of nature. That's why I'm so interested in Alaska."

And that's why it's not surprising that only a Red Berenson can get excited about nothing more than a canoe. He takes what amounts to a paternal interest in his canoe. "It means something to me," he explains. "It's something special in our lives, not the way it might be for the average person. We respect it."

Similarly, opponents and teammates respect Red Berenson. They respect his consummate skating ability, his creative stickhandling and the fact that he has developed into one of the genuine stars of the West Division. After the Rangers traded him to St. Louis for Ron Stewart early in the 1967-68 season, Berenson emerged as the superb hockey player critics have expected him to be all these years. In 55 games with the Blues he scored 22 goals and 29 assists for a total of 51 points, which put him ahead of such names as Frank Mahovlich, Ron Ellis and Dave Keon.

There are those who will suggest that Berenson's intellect—he has a B.A. from the University of Michigan—helps his game. He's not so sure. "It's hard to measure the amount of thinking a man will do off ice and then in a game. In hockey there isn't the time to think that one has in a planned game like football and baseball; in hockey we do things instinctively more often. Men who seem quite ignorant off the ice turn out to be very smart hockey players.

"Some intelligent players who do too much thinking on the ice ruin their game. Then you have a player like Doug Harvey (an ex-Blues defenseman) who was smart and knew how to relax in a hectic game. He was so good at it he could calm the whole game down if he wanted to."

Berenson's good head wasn't always appreciated. Montreal's Toe Blake underplayed Red when Blake coached the Canadiens and Berenson insists he never got a good chance to prove himself with Les Canadiens. "I was a different kind of player compared to the ones Blake was accustomed to. He knew I was a college man—not that I consider myself an intellectual, I don't—and I don't think he believed I could make it. When your coach is thinking that way, your chances are not too good."

But Berenson hardly saw more ice when he was traded to the Rangers. At first it seemed he'd be the number one center but an injury sidelined him and his place was taken by Orland Kurtenbach; every time he made a comeback he'd suffer another injury and the word—unfairly—made the rounds that he was brittle.

Curiously, most of Berenson's major excitement occurred off the ice when he was a Ranger. For example, there was the time he and a friend went out in a 26-foot motorboat for a spin in the Atlantic Ocean off Long Island. By the time the little vessel made it into the deeper part of the ocean the motor conked out. It hardly looked promising for Red and friend.

"There's fog," he recalls, "and I'm seasick, and here's my pal sitting in the stern lapping up brandy. There's no oars and no anchor. Twice out of the fog there comes ocean-going craft that miss us by less than 30 feet."

The odyssey had a happy ending. After priming the engine several dozen times, Red finally got it to work and eventually steered the craft safely back to shore. By now it is almost imperative that a hockey team take out boat wreckage insurance for Berenson because his affinity for boats—and boating disasters—is worrisome.

Another time he went out fishing in one of his favorite camp areas in a distant sector of British Columbia. He was accompanied by Don Miller, a sales representative, and they were making their way in a small dinghy no more than 12 feet long. Here's how the saga unfolded in Berenson's own words:

"We had a 10-horsepower motor on the back, which is pretty monstrous power for such a little boat. All of a sudden, the motor exploded off the back of the boat and tore off the end. Water poured in. This was a mountain lake fed by glaciers. Very cold. Mountains pitched down to the surface, which means there wasn't much shore."

To save themselves, the men moved to the front of the boat, keeping it partially afloat. They had one lifejacket and one paddle. Nothing else.

"I can swim," adds Berenson, "but we were 50 yards from shore and I'd heard that in water that cold you couldn't survive more than three or five minutes. So I picked up the oar and began paddling—furious as hell! But we started drifting toward a 70-foot waterfall. I wasn't scared at the time, that came later, but all I was thinking about was paddle, paddle. At last we managed to angle away from the falls. We got near to shore and, as things turned out, the only thing I got was wet feet, and sweat from paddling."

Before they could retrieve the motor it sank. The next day a diver was summoned as part of a salvage operation. When Berenson remembers what happened next a shiver or two curls up his back. "Before the diver was to go down, they put a rock on a rope to measure how deep the lake was. The rock went down *400* feet without touching bottom, so the salvage operation was called off."

GERRY CHEEVERS

If Puck's Bad Boy had been a goaltender, he would have been named Gerry Cheevers.

The Boston Bruins' blond goalie plays it like a combination forward-defenseman and occasional goaltender.

Late last season in a crucial game against the Detroit Red Wings he intercepted the puck and skated all the way to center ice as if he were about to take a shot on the Red Wing net.

Many times during the hectic 1970 race he exchanged stick-slashes, body-bumps and insults with opposing forwards, much in the manner of his tough backline colleagues.

And, of course, Cheevers was there to play goal. He performed this chore in his usual flamboyant way, which means he sometimes is the worst in the business. But, more often, he can be called the best—as he was in the Stanley Cup playoffs last spring when he helped pace Boston to the Stanley Cup.

Gerry Cheevers is the most outspoken and colorful goaltender of any of the 24 chaps who regularly stop the 100 mile per hour shots in hockey's major league.

He is also the only goaltender who happens to be an expert on training race horses and who someday expects to groom a winner in the Kentucky Derby or, at the very least, The Queen's Plate of Canada, the premier race north of the border.

All of which has helped combine to make Cheevers one of the most unusual personalities in hockey and one of the most outspoken since Jacques Plante played for the Montreal Canadiens.

The 30-year-old Cheevers takes himself a little less seriously than other goalies. And he has an excellent outlet for his emotions in horse racing.

"I've been around the track about 15 years," he explained. "First it was Fort Erie, Ontario, then Woodbine, near Toronto. I like racing because of the people and the thoroughbred race horse. I think it's the greatest thing in the world."

Cheevers' interest in the track developed during his teenage days in his hometown of St. Catherines, Ontario, where he became friends with a horse trainer named Bob Warner. Gerry has been a racing fanatic ever since.

"Warner knew I was a junior goalie at the time," Gerry recalled, "and he loved hockey. He once explained to me that a stable was trained the way a hockey team was coached. That is, every horse is different and has to be treated that way.

"A young horse, like a rookie player, has to be worked hard and taught how to run. In other words, you play hockey the way the manager wants you to play and you play sound hockey.

" 'A fat horse,' he'd say, possibly referring to me because I tend to get overweight, 'has to be put in shape and kept in shape; like the long lengthy workouts in horseracing.' The comparison with hockey is that a fat guy will get more pressure from the coach and he'll have to do something extra on the ice after the workout."

During the non-hockey months Cheevers does racing public relations and conducts interviews at the track. His mind is so organized that he now inevitably makes comparisons between hockey and racing.

"There are horses," he went on, "that have to be pampered the way some hockey players have to be babied. When I was playing minor league hockey in Rochester, my coach was Joe Crozier. He was one of the best coaches I've ever played with and he had to pamper me.

"Then, you have the stake horses in racing and the stake horses in hockey. In hockey they're Bobby Orr and Phil Esposito. They'll run their own race. I don't think they can have any disturbance from the management or the coach."

One of Cheevers' ambitions is to write a novel about racing. He's already penned a few chapters on the long plane rides from the East to the West coast and back.

"I've always felt that a thoroughbred was worth studying. And race-trackers are the most down-to-earth, honest and fairest people I've ever met."

According to Gerry, he'll remain in hockey "until they stop issuing me pads at training camp," but his interest in racing will continue long after that.

"I've got a dream," he said. "It's something that comes up every two or three days of my life. I want to train a champion thoroughbred. Mind you, not own one, but train one. But that won't happen until hockey is finished."

At the rate both Cheevers and the Bruins are going it doesn't appear that his hockey days will be over for another decade.

"I'm not highstrung like a lot of other NHL goalies," said Cheevers. "I consider myself carefree and that's one reason I avoid tension. But actually I have deep thoughts on everything."

Including himself.

"As far as my own playing is concerned there's a lot of room for improvement. I have no set pattern of goaltending. I'm not a stand-up type and I'm not a flopper. I might do either one in a particular situation. I have a lot of confidence in my stick and my ability to skate.

"I've always had hopes of being an Ed Giacomin or a Glenn Hall or a Jacques Plante. I've given myself enough years to reach these goals and I've never panicked. It takes time for a goaltender to develop; in our business experience is the the greatest thing in the world. I've often said to myself, if I reach thirty or thirty-two and I haven't really made it in the NHL then it's time to start panicking and thinking of something else to do. But I've proven I can play here. Now the job is to maintain the right mental attitude."

Since Cheevers admittedly isn't the best in the NHL, the logical question remains: who is his superior—Tony Esposito, Rogatien Vachon, Ed Giacomin?

The way Gerry sees it Giacomin is the top man in the business today.

"I know I'm not his equal," Cheevers asserted, "because the records prove this. He's played a lot more games than I have and he has more experience. He does everything well and he's especially good with his stick and his skating. I think if any goaltender is going to score a goal in this game it'll be Eddie first and me second."

One of Giacomin's fortes is his propensity for keeping a "book" on his opponents. After each game the Ranger goalie adds a few notes on each player who gave him trouble. Giacomin contends that his volumes have been of immeasurable aid in improving his game. Cheevers, by contrast, keeps no such "book" on the enemy.

"I keep everything I learn about the opposition in my mind," Gerry said. "If I see a player like Bill Fairbairn (of the Rangers) shooting twice in the same place—to the top corner—I'll remember that and be sure to cover up the next time. For example, I can go over players on the Rangers and tell you all about them.

"Take Jean Ratelle. He's got a great shift and an excellent wrist shot. Vic Hadfield has the best knuckle ball in the league. He uses a curved stick and the puck does all kinds of tricks when he shoots.

Sports came easy to Cheevers. His father was a noted lacrosse player; so good, in fact, he became a member of Canada's Lacrosse Hall of Fame. His dad also was a scout for the Toronto Maple Leafs, a fact that amuses Gerry these days.

"I think they fired him when they found out I was the only guy he scouted."

Cheevers moved up the Leaf chain and might very well have become Toronto's number one goaltender today were it not for the fact that the Leafs had Johnny Bower in the nets during Cheevers' developing days. In time the Bruins picked him up and Gerry matured on their Oklahoma City franchise before being promoted to the NHL.

Last year Cheevers split the goaltending assignment with Ed Johnston. According to coach Harry Sinden's plan, Cheevers worked one night and Johnston the next.

"Harry made it clear at the beginning of the season that the system would be exactly equal and there'd be no change. I think it's a very fair system if you have two equal goaltenders. And, in my opinion, I'm playing the best hockey of my life so I really can't knock the system. Besides, Eddie and I are the best of friends and have a lot of respect for each other. I don't think we would want it any other way.

"Eddie and I have played together for many years and I think I know him better than anyone; you couldn't pick a better guy to play with. He's 100 per cent for the team. He studies the game and he isn't bashful about telling me what I'm doing wrong."

There's another line of thinking among goalies that says one man—in the Rangers' case it's Giacomin—should play as much as possible. Cheevers disagrees.

"In the hockey of this day and age no goalie is capable of playing all the games. When I broke into the NHL it was different. Johnny Bower was playing 70 games for the Leafs; but he was a glutton for punishment."

Having studied the art of goaltending since he arrived in the NHL, Cheevers believes he has worked out the formula for determining the perfect netminder. It goes this way:

"Start with the scientific and mechanical skills of Jacques Plante. He plays goal like a machine and doesn't make any mistakes. Then add the quickness of Glenn Hall. He's the fastest and doesn't do many things right. He's the most unorthodox goalie. Then, take the patience and attitude of Gump Worsley.

"From there you go to the agility of Roger Crozier. He can be caught out of position but he can get back into position because of his agility. Then, conclude with the natural talent and skating ability of Giacomin and the old clutch play Terry Sawchuk had and you have the perfect goalie."

Someday that perfect goalie may be Gerry Cheevers.

PHIL ESPOSITO

Contrary to what one might gather from the newspapers there are other players on the Boston Bruins besides Bobby Orr. What's more, there are others who win hockey games and one such skater is sloe-eyed Phil Esposito, who just happened to finish second in scoring behind the indescribable Orr.

Although it sounds like ancient history now it is this very same Esposito who set a league scoring record with 126 points in the 1968-69 season and who "slumped" to 99 points last year. Among the Boston forwards, Esposito leads the attack and proved it in the playoffs as well as the regular season last year when he was picked to the First All-Star team.

He scored a three-goal hat trick in the Bruins opening game against the Rangers during the first round of the

Stanley Cup playoffs last April and then rescued the Boston sextet in the decisive fifth game of the series when the teams were tied at two games apiece. The Rangers were leading 2-1 early in the third period when Esposito tied the score and then, minutes later, scored what proved to be the winning goal.

"Phil," said ex-Bruin Red Sullivan, "is one of the great all-time players in front of the net. He has the moves. He always comes up with the puck." He continued to excel against Chicago and St. Louis as the Bruins romped to their first Stanley Cup win in 29 years.

A veteran Boston hockey authority added: "When Espo's line is skating and digging and throwing its weight around it can't be stopped."

In his record-breaking year Esposito played alongside Ken Hodge and Ron Murphy. When Murphy retired last season tall, tough Wayne Cashman was added to the line. "Those two guys are great in the corners," credits Phil. "They want me to be backing up the play. We don't want to get three men caught in deep."

At first glance Esposito suggests a nonchalance bordering on "I don't give a damn." Actually he can take a very serious turn; especially at playoff time, as he proved last season. "I've been in the playoffs six years in a row and I still get excited before every opening game," said Phil. "I try not to let it bother me, but it does. I have trouble getting to sleep. I think about what we have to do."

He's also superstitious. If he notices any sticks lying atop other sticks, he'll straighten out the stack. "I just don't like to see crossed sticks," he admits. "It bugs me." Likewise, he always puts his left shin pad on first and then the left skate; and he wears a St. Christopher medal inside his heavy hockey pants.

Needless to say, superstition is not the key to Esposito's success. Teammate Ed Westfall contends that 'showmanship' is the reason.

Showmanship? Here's how the articulate Westfall dissects his man:

"What it boils down to is Espo's great deception; when he's coming up the ice, he shows the puck to the other team's defenseman. Now this defenseman might have every intention of trying to bodycheck Espo, but once he sees the puck, it takes his mind off hitting him.

"Espo's moving nice and slow, and the next thing the other guy knows, Phil is by him. Espo may look cumbersome and slow, but he's deceiving. He's so strong that many times he'll beat the other guy by four or five feet. The only other guy on the club who can do these kinds of things is Bobby Orr."

If Espo had been inducted in the U.S. Army the chances are that doctors would have quickly signed the discharge papers—after looking at his feet.

"Let's just say," Phil mentioned later, "that I make the supreme sacrifice any time I stop a shot with my foot...my father has bad feet. Would you believe his feet scarcely touch the ground?"

Then, a pause: "I've decided my trouble came from wearing my own skates. You see, I used to wear size tens. They hurt my feet; one day I picked up a pair of Red Kelly's skates. I mean they were made to order for him. When I tried them on, they felt great. I've been wearing them ever since."

Espo admits he didn't think it was very funny when he was traded by the flying Hawks to the Bruins three years ago. Boston had been last the previous year but he knew he was with a good hockey team and told coach Sinden so.

"What I missed first was Bobby Hull and Chico Maki," said Espo. "We were pretty close. One night in a game in Boston I had to hook Bobby to stop him from getting a goal. He winds up in the net. I wind up against the boards. At the time we were in front 7-2. To make matters worse, I get a penalty—only my second of the season. Bobby said, 'You big dumb oaf, are you trying to get us both killed?' What I should have done was tackle him, I guess."

Mostly, though, it's the other guys who are trying to tackle Espo. Their efforts have been inept to say the least and that explains why the sloe-eyed center with the wry grin is known as the "Espo Express." The Bruins' newly hired bench coach, Tom Johnson, put it this way: "In the old days when we played shinny on a river, Espo would be the guy with the puck all the time."

At the start of the 1968-69 season Bobby Orr was the glamour boy in Boston but Espo's record-breaking effort moved him up on the popularity poll. "I got about 50 letters a week," he said. "It's unreal."

Phil claims he wasn't aware of his record-breaking potential until the night of February 5, 1969. "That's when I scored two goals and two assists and it brought me up to 82 points," he recalls. "A week later in Boston I got five points against Chicago and I was sure I had a shot at it."

In some quarters Esposito had been criticized for being "point-hungry." That description is pinned on players—most often on stars—who badger game officials for extra assists on scoring plays. After a while they begin to pile up and add to a skater's bargaining potential when he deals with his manager over a new contract. Boston Garden had a character not long ago who needled Espo as a "hungry" for points type of player; especially when Phil squawked to the Bruins' official scorer.

"If I deserve a point," Espo countered, "then I expect the scorer to give it to me. I just want to win the game. I don't care that much who scores or who gets the points. As long as we win I feel I've contributed. It doesn't matter if I get one point or 20."

Judging by his production in the past few years, Esposito should be among the leading scorers throughout the Seventies.

TONY ESPOSITO

One of the biggest laughs heard around the National Hockey League in October 1969 emanated from Chicago where the Black Hawks announced that Tony Esposito would be their starting goaltender. This was most amusing to shinny birddogs since it had been quite obvious only a season earlier that the bulky brother of Phil Esposito couldn't even make it with the Montreal Canadiens. And, if a goaltender couldn't cut it with the then Stanley Cup champions, where would he make it?

Obviously, Black Hawk manager Tommy Ivan believed that 27-year-old Tony had the goods. He relegated veteran Denis DeJordy to the bench and decided to go with Esposito come hell or high water. For several weeks it was pure hell for the Hawks. They were cemented to the second division and seemed incapable of better things when, all of a sudden, Tony Esposito started playing the kind of goal that astonished the hockey world around him. By mid-season he had seven shutouts and the Hawks were contenders again.

"I've been lucky," said Tony. "In a couple of those shutouts, a shot or two bounced off the post. Besides, a shutout means a complete team defensive effort."

The Black Hawks experienced a complete strategic metamorphosis when Esposito went into the nets. Once the scoring wonders of hockey, they now stressed defense and more defense. It was a completely different team from the one Tony faced when he played for the Canadiens.

"Either I didn't see the Hawks properly from the other end of the net or it was a different team this year," said Tony. "I'd have to say it was a different team. No one, I don't care who, could have that many shutouts without a team like this in front. Hockey has become so wide open that the first team that turned it around had a good chance of winning. We were the first, I guess."

While Tony was taking dead aim at the Vezina Trophy, brother Phil was running strong for his second straight scoring championship. This, of course, meant that the two Espositos were on collision course eight times during the season. "If I made a save on Phil," Tony recalled, "he'd crack afterwards that I was lucky, but we don't kibitz in a game. That's all business. Off the ice it's a lot of fun needling each other but on the ice there's no way Phil's going to score if I can prevent it."

During the regular 1969-70 campaign Tony allowed Phil only two out of his league-leading 43 goals. But in the very first game of the Boston-Chicago Stanley Cup East

Division final Phil produced a three-goal hat trick. "His defense was not as good as it had been," said Phil. "Besides, he had robbed me blind during the regular season." The Bruins blasted Tony out of the playoffs in four games, although he did manage to rob Phil in the final match.

Phil wasn't the only one robbed by Tony. The Michigan Tech graduate managed a record-breaking 15 shutouts, topping the NHL team mark of 13 shared by three clubs. His 2.17 goals against average for 63 games was regarded as substantial evidence for Tony to win the Hart Trophy as the league's MVP. "There's no question," said team-mate Bobby Hull, "that Tony is the most valuable man." However, Bobby Orr of Boston won the Hart, so Tony had to be content with the rookie award and a berth on the All-Star Team.

At first look Tony appears to be a clumsy goaltender whose most notable asset is luck. This, however, was the same observation once made about Johnny Bower, who starred for so many years in the Toronto net. Montreal Gazette columnist Ted Blackman once queried goalies Gump Worsley and Gerry Desjardins about Esposito and came up with a couple of interesting insights. Worsley, to begin with, had teamed with Esposito on the 1968-69 Cup-winning Canadiens.

"He's a solid goaltender," Worsley told Blackman. "His only weakness is long shots. He can't see, wears contact lenses and still can't see those outside shots. But he's dynamite in close. When you're on top of him you haven't much chance."

Desjardins, who was traded by Los Angeles to Chicago late last season, enjoyed an interesting perspective on Tony from the Hawk bench. "I've never seen a goalie do the things he can do," said Desjardins. "He has a way of dropping to his knees and spreading his pads out to either side on certain kinds of shots, mostly from the point. That way he's in better shape to take care of rebounds than I am after I've done the splits on the same shots.

"Another great thing he does is give the shooter a target between his pads then drop down at the last second to close it off. It requires great timing and he has it down perfectly. His timing is terrific and he always seems to know exactly where the puck is, even with his back turned."

Esposito's climb to the NHL has been as unlikely as his goaltending. At home in Sault Ste. Marie, Ontario, he played center for the local team. He quit hockey for more than a year when he was 18 and then resumed playing in a position he loathed—goal.

"They needed a goaltender and they kept harrassing me," he once told Paul Rimstead, sports editor of *The Canadian Magazine*. "I didn't want to play. I don't like it. It's no fun playin' goal, y'know. There's the pressure and everything. I still don't like it."

When Tony was 19 he received a scholarship to Michigan Tech where he eventually became an All-American and graduated with a business degree. In time he received a letter from the Canadiens, inviting him to their training camp. It was a pleasant surprise. "I don't know how they got my professional rights," he explained. "I was on one of the stupid lists or something."

The Canadiens dispatched him to Vancouver of the Western League in 1967-68. It was a conspicuously inferior team and, as a result, an excellent place for a young goaltender to learn his trade. "I learned all about losing that season," said Tony, "and how I really didn't enjoy it."

A year later Tony was playing for Houston in the Central League when injuries to Worsley and Rogatien Vachon compelled the Canadiens to bring Esposito to the NHL. He played in 13 games and emerged with a 2.73 average. While he was at it he produced two shutouts which meant that mathematically he would have hit for a near-record 11 had he played an entire season.

Somehow this factor eluded Montreal's general manager Sam Pollock. When it came time to protect players in the 1969 draft Pollock covered Worsley, Vachon and young Phil Myre. It proved to be one of the classic mistakes committed by Pollock, who is not known for his faux pas. In retrospect Pollock has argued that Esposito never would have played as well for the 1969-70 Canadiens as he did for the Black Hawks. "He wouldn't have had 15 shutouts playing behind the Canadiens," Pollock insists.

That, of course, remains debatable, just as it is uncertain how well Esposito can guard the nets now that the

NHL shooters have had a full season in which to study his style. There are those who believe he will be solved this season—as he was solved by the Bruins in the playoffs—and the Esposito myth will burst as quickly as it inflated. There are others who envision Esposito going on and on and on, just like Bower did with the Maple Leafs.

"He's like Bower was when I was with Toronto," said teammate Jim Pappin. "He doesn't even want you to score on him in practice."

The younger Esposito is a first-class competitor who admits he won't even play a game of golf for relaxation. "I don't like to play *ANY* sport for relaxation," he says. "I go out to win."

There wasn't a goalie who could do it better in 1969-70.

JOHN FERGUSON

The figures surrounding John Ferguson last season were deceptive.

Montreal's boisterous left wing scored only 19 goals and 13 assists for 32 points. A season earlier he had an impressive 29-23-52. Was it true that Ferguson was washed up?

Certainly.

Ferguson suffered a broken cheekbone, broken thumb, a depressing assortment of minor injuries and a suspension. When all the contusions and abrasions were totalled up they accounted for 28 full games lost by Ferguson and one of the essential reasons why the Canadiens missed a playoff berth for the first time since 1948.

"One man can make a big difference to a team," said Montreal's general manager Sam Pollock. But few players meant so much to a team as Ferguson to Les Canadiens. He supplies the sock and the inspiration, and when he's gone it's like a trombone without its slide. And if you ask the 32-year-old strongboy he'll tell you there's only one way to play the game.

"Tough and hard," says Ferguson. "Take your knocks and bruises. That's the only way to win. I'll give you an example: we were playing Toronto late last season when the Leaf goalie Bruce Gamble made a save. Gamble had the puck in his pads but the whistle hadn't blown. I crashed him to knock it loose and in the scramble Ralph Backstrom got it into the net. You've got to play it that way."

Coach Claude Ruel agrees. "In the room," says Ruel, "before the game and between periods, that Fergie makes a difference. He talks and yells and makes them listen and makes them mad. He's so honest and he isn't shy. He'll tell a guy just what he thinks and the guy listens. Fergie is so honest and he wants everybody else to be honest when they play."

When he's not brawling and yelling, Big, Bad John usually is scoring; and when he puts his mind to it, he does it better than most skaters.

To the casual observer, Ferguson as a scorer is completely out of character. His image is that of "Heavyweight Champ of Hockey," a title unofficially bestowed on him last season by *Toronto Daily Star* author Trent Frayne. It is based on victories over Kent Douglas, Ted Green, Reg Fleming, Eddie Shack and several others not known for their timidity. But, as Detroit's bruising Bob Baun once told me, "There's always somebody around who will beat the guy who's beating everybody."

And so it was that Fleming came back at Ferguson in the 1969 playoffs and emerged with at least a draw. Then Green's Boston linemate, Don Awrey, tangled with the Canadien bulldozer in the final game and also held his own, if he didn't actually win it on points. What's significant—and symbolic—about the Awrey episode is that Fergie may have lost the battle but he won the war, with his scoring stick.

It was Fergie who pursued Awrey behind the net in the second sudden death overtime in April 1969 and forced the Bruin to make a wild pass that ultimately landed on Claude Provost's stick. Provost then sidestepped the charging Awrey and put the puck where Beliveau wanted it and Beliveau put it in.

"Sometimes," said Fergie in a moment of selfexamination, "I wonder about the fights. They take a lot out of you and keep a guy from doing his real job—the scoring."

He has come to understand that hard work has given him a potent forehand shot and persistence has rewarded him with a skating style that puts him on a par with some of the better sprinters, if not the best. To those who knew him as a young player, this is virtually impossible to believe. Jack Gordon, the new coach of the Minnesota North Stars, is one of them.

"I signed Fergie in 1960-61," Gordon recalled, "and he was just an awful-looking player at the time, even by American League standards. He'd fight the puck and lose it. And his skating was awkward. But the thing I liked about him was that he'd fight like the devil to get it back."

Aldo Guidolin, a scout for the Baltimore Clippers, was a teammate of Ferguson's at the time. "He's got to go all the way to the NHL," said Guidolin.

It took three seasons in the AHL for Ferguson to hone his style to NHL sharpness. The Rangers had eyes on him, but the Canadiens got to him first and he was signed in the 1963-64 season. A year earlier the Montrealers had finished first and have done so three more times since. They never have dropped below second once since Fergie's worn the bleu (blue), blanc (white), et rouge (and red) jersey.

During that inflationary period Fergie has been cautioned about his exuberance. Management believed that some of his penalties were not only unnecessary, they were detrimental to the game. He was warned to cool it and he did. As a result, the Canadiens—and Ferguson—suffered even more. This was in 1967 and the Habs had slipped to an unlikely fifth place for a week or so.

"I had to take stock," said Fergie. "I could see the new approach wasn't working."

In a matter of weeks the Canadiens had revived themselves and climbed right up to second place.

Opponents have discovered that Fergie's weakness is tranquility. When they observe truce regulations, they often lull him into passivity and his game deteriorates.

"I just wish that every time a game starts somebody would take a crack at me," the 5'11", 190-pounder admitted. "It sort of sets me in the right mood."

Off-ice, his mood is somewhere between suave and ministerial. Ferguson cultivates flowers, trains trotters and works in the public relations department of Blue Bonnets race track in Montreal. One afternoon my wife and I were having lunch with Fergie. She had taken a cigarette out of a pack; Fergie softly took the match from her hand and simultaneously lit her cigarette with his butane lighter. Maurice Chevalier couldn't have done it more gallantly.

Of course, he wouldn't be so courteous to an opponent. In fact, he refuses to attend off-season banquets, speak to or be seen with members of the loyal opposition. Once he dropped into a Toronto restaurant for dinner and as the waitress brought over the menu, he noticed a couple of Toronto Maple Leaf players at a nearby table. He excused himself to the waitress and walked out.

"There's no sense being two-faced," he asserted. "We'd have to speak, those guys and me. Talking to a man one minute and trying to knock the daylights out of him the next is no good."

The case of Ferguson inspires a question—how does a hockey fighter get that way: In his case the answer is as direct as one of his punches. When Johnny was a kid growing up in Vancouver British Columbia, he got a job as stickboy for the Vancouver Canucks of the Western Hockey League. One night the Canucks were playing the Edmonton Flyers and high-scoring Phil Maloney, Vancouver's little center, became embroiled in a fight with Edmonton's big, tough defenseman, Larry Zeidel. And it all happened in front of Fergie at the Vancouver bench.

"Zeidel sneaked up on him from behind," said Fergie. "He just killed Maloney. Phil almost lost an eye. I stood there and looked at the other players on that Vancouver team. Not one guy went to help. I hated that whole team. I made up my mind that if I ever became a hockey player I'd never stand by and watch something like that happen to one of my teammates."

Sure enough, Ferguson eventually graduated to Cleveland of the American League where he found himself face-to-face with Zeidel who played for Hershey. Unaware of Fergie's feelings, Zeidel was taken aback when John vaulted the boards, headed straight for him and then flailed him with punches. "Yeah," said Ferguson, "I gave him a few for Phil."

It didn't take long for word of Fergie's pugilistic ability to get around the American League. But it took three seasons before any NHL team was willing to gamble on him. The Canadiens finally did, just ahead of the Rangers, and brought him to training camp in the fall of 1963. "We didn't really know what we were getting," recalled Montreal's general manager, Sam Pollock. "We'd heard he was a man who wasn't reluctant to mix it up. But he turned out to be a surprise . . . a happy one for us." Judging by John Ferguson's performances in Montreal, the feeling is mutual.

GORDIE HOWE

Gordie Howe is like a fisherman who made a great catch and, then, heading back to port let his net remain in the sea. By the time he reached shore the net was overflowing with a still greater catch.

So it is with hockey's alter-ego. Howe has done everything an athlete can be expected to do; over and over and over again. At 42 he is now in his 25th National Hockey League season. Every time he plays in a game, scores a goal, receives an assist or is handed a penalty, Howe sets a record.

He is a mental and physical marvel whose feats very likely will never be duplicated. No player ever displayed more courage under more trying conditions. Last season, for example, he was plagued from the start of training camp in September until the playoffs in April with an arthritic wrist and assorted other injuries. Yet he played in all 76 regular season games and all playoff contests. What's more, he scored 31 goals and 40 assists for 71 points to lead the Red Wings in scoring. He placed ninth in the NHL scoring race ahead of such younger stars as Bobby Hull, Yvan Cournoyer and Dave Keon and was named to the first All-Star Team at right wing.

With each season it becomes more and more apparent that Howe is the greatest all-round hockey player who ever lived. Maurice Richard thinks so and Bobby Hull thinks so and those are among the best who've ever laced on a pair of skates. "When the guys are sitting around the dressing room talking about who we're going to play," says Hull, "they'll say, 'Well, tomorrow night Montreal, Toronto on Saturday and Gordie on Sunday'."

Like Richard and other great ones, Hull and Howe wear number nine. Prior to the All-Star Game in Montreal in 1969 Hull arrived in the dressing room of The Forum. The tape above his locker was scribbled, "Hull. No. 16." And that's the number Hull knew belonged to him that night.

"He knows," said *Detroit Free Press* sports editor Joe Falls, "just as everyone in the NHL knows: there is only one Number Nine."

The reasons are all there in the record book which Howe practically owns—most years, most games, most goals, most assists, most points. "He dominates the game," says *Windsor Star* hockey writer Jack Dulmage, "as no player has dominated it. He goes anywhere and everywhere and allows no one to take liberties with him. His greatness extends to every avenue of play."

And then some.

Howe's behavior is condemned for its roughness and condoned for its naturalness in the NHL jungle.

"He has his detractors who claim he is dirty," says Dulmage. "It is not much of a valid claim. Howe plays as roughly or cleanly as the circumstances require."

To me," added Joe Falls, "it's good, clean, hard hockey."

The years may have tired him somewhat, but they certainly haven't mellowed the man who has the reputation for being one of the meanest hitters in hockey. Along the player's grapevine the word is that it's not smart to cross Gordie; and if you do cross him, be sure you keep your eyes open because, sooner or later, he's going to get you back—in spades.

Mike Walton, a center for the Maple Leafs, and Howe clashed during the 1968 All Star Game at Maple Leaf Gardens in Toronto. "In an irrational moment," wrote George Gross in the Toronto *Telegram*, "Walton undertook a kamikaze assignment—challenging Howe to a fight. Howe tripped Walton and the latter decided to take on the Detroit right-winger, whose specialty over the years has been carving the mark of Zorro on his opponents."

Linesmen broke up the impending battle just as Howe was moving in on Walton, a fact that displeased Gordie no end. "So he (Walton) doesn't like to get hit, eh?" he observed later. "I stuck my hip out and dumped him. He came up swinging at my head. We'll see how tough he is the next time. I didn't do anything to him tonight. Why, I almost kissed him in the ear."

Off-ice Howe has been the epitome of sweetness and light. One night in Montreal a crippled child was introduced to him prior to a game at The Forum against the Canadiens. "I'll get one for you tonight," Gordie promised. An hour later he had beaten Rogatien Vachon in the Montreal net. Howe hadn't forgotten. He dove into the webbing, retrieved the rubber and presented it to the youngster after the game.

This is matter-of-fact stuff with Howe. Once he drove 20 miles out of his way late at night to give a man an autograph he had promised—but had forgotten—for his child. Many times he makes unpublicized visits to hospitals to cheer the infirm.

He is a remarkable athlete and his greatness presents the Red Wings with an enormous problem they have been able to avert lo these many years—what will they do when Gordie Howe eventually does retire as he threatens to do at the end of this season?

There apparently is no answer to the question.

BOBBY HULL

For Bobby Hull the 1969-70 season was both depressing and ecstatic. It was the year that he had his most bitter clash with management and missed the first 14 games of the campaign. He was replaced as hockey's premier glamour boy by Bobby Orr of the Bruins. Nevertheless he helped Chicago to first place in the East and won a place on the All-Star Team.

The Black Hawk brass made it clear when Hull returned in the Autumn of 1969 that he would do things their way or he wouldn't do them at all. It was a demeaning command but it was one that Hull chose to obey and, as a result, everyone connected with Chicago hockey was the better for it: Hull, the Hawks and management.

Bobby was ordered by the high command to be as zealous with his backchecking and defensive play as he was with his scoring. He was informed that he no longer would be excused from practices for personal appearances and non-hockey business. He was told very succinctly that he was just another member of the Chicago sextet and there would be no exception to that rule.

Hull accepted the new status quo and his adaptation to the role of Mister Defense developed into one of the most arresting tales of the 1969-70 season. With Bobby back in the lineup the Hawks climbed into contention and stunned the hockey world by beating out the favored Bruins to finish in first place in the NHL's East Division.

"Bobby Hull no longer is the Golden Jet, the whirling fusilier who averaged 52 goals per season over the last four years," observed Jerry Green in *The Detroit News*. "He is better, and more valuable as a hockey player."

The proof was in the standings. During the 1968-69 season Hull scored a record 58 goals but Chicago finished in last place. A year later Bobby scored 20 fewer goals but the Black Hawks owned The Prince of Wales Trophy.

"Bobby got 38 goals," said Black Hawk coach Billy Reay, "and had his best season in all-around play. After being out at the beginning of the season Hull realized how we were playing and adapted."

The adaptation did not come easily. At first critics around the NHL insisted that Reay was making a large mistake trying to convert Hull who, at 31, was in his 13th season with Chicago. Bobby, himself, offered several disparaging remarks about how he couldn't play the defensive game as well.

"It took me to the first of the year to feel like a hockey player again," said Bobby. "But it's easy when everyone goes all-out, not two or three guys one night and two or three the next. It was a different kind of a season, a very gratifying season.

"We were determined to play better defensively. There were so many kids trying to make the team and they knew they had to play good defense, so everyone caught on to the new style. 'From adversity comes good,' to quote an old saying of my former coach, Rudy Pilous."

A key to Reay's revised strategy was to align Hull with two renowned defensive players, Eric Nesterenko and Chico Maki. The system worked to perfection through the remainder of the season and in the opening round of the playoffs when Chicago wiped out the Detroit Red Wings in four straight games. Nesterenko guarded Frank Mahovlich of the Wings and Hull took good care of Gordie Howe. While the Red Wings were buried, Bobby led the series in scoring with three goals and six assists.

This proved rather conclusively that it still was necessary for opponents to shadow Hull with one of their better defensive players because at any given time Bobby could bust out with a spate of key goals. The Bruins shadowed Hull with Ed Westfall in the East Division finals and that time Bobby struck out.

Hull's shadows fall into two categories. The first is the group of clean defensive players who will avoid fouling Hull as much as possible in their attempts to defend against him. The second is the collection of players who are less than scrupulous in following the rulebook. Bryan

Watson is the most notorious of those shadows because of an episode that occurred a few years ago when Watson played for the Detroit Red Wings.

The Black Hawks had just scored against Detroit and it appeared that the puck either was put in by Hull or that it went in off a Red Wings' skate. "That's not your goal," Watson needled Hull. "The puck hit me. It's (Phil) Esposito's goal. Be a big man, give it to Esposito."

Watson's persistent chatter was getting to Hull but it wasn't 'til later in the game that he really hit a nerve. Watson raced up from behind and laid the lumber on the Golden Jet. Hull went down but not for long. He got to his feet in a few seconds and, suddenly, swung his stick over Watson's head. "My stick came around," said Hull, "and I clunked him."

It was an act of war not in the Hull tradition and he paid for it. Sid Abel, then general manager and coach of the Red Wings, laced into Hull unmercifully, as did several other Detroit players. After the game Hull walked to the medical room where a doctor was lacing 18 stitches into Watson's wound. "I meant to hit you," said Hull, "but I didn't mean to maim you."

Watson looked up, hardly mollified and shot back: "It's a long season."

But Watson wasn't the only one. Ed Westfall of the Bruins, Reg Fleming, of the Philadelphia Flyers, and several other checkers have given Hull the business and, mostly, he's taken it without reprisal.

"They take advantage of him," said goalie Glenn Hall.

Bobby's father is hulking Robert, now 60, who was a mill foreman at the Canada Cement Plant in Point Anne, Ontario, when Bobby was growing up. Bobby's father has remained an ardent fan and when he talks about Bobby, he calls him Robert, and appreciates his love of the land as well as his hockey.

On the farm there's nothing Bobby will not do. He fixes fences, re-seeds the meadows, plants corn and oats and hay, drives tractors, plows and combines and pitches hay. "I'm a country boy at heart," he has said.

But hockey fans are not really that interested in Hull the farmer. They want him to score goals and more goals —despite Reay's strategy—and in 1968-69 he obliged to the point of breaking his old record of 54 goals scored in the 1965-66 season. Part of his success has been in learning to pace himself, to move when he has to move, the way Gordie Howe has done it.

"You don't waste energy," he said. "You pick your spots and you go when you know you have the edge. It's an instinct. You get so that you can anticipate when you should outrace or outbody or outmaneuver. You sense your opening and you react. There's a lot in knowing what you yourself can do. If you see an opening something tells you if you can make it or not make it."

More than most other players in hockey Bobby Hull makes it. In fact, he makes it whether he's on the rink, or in an ad office or simply signing autograph after autograph until his hand is so tired he can't write anymore.

"Listen," he'll say, "if they're interested enough in staying and waiting for my autograph, I'll keep signing. I look at it this way—when I stop enjoying hockey and it becomes hard work, then I'll put the skates away."

DAVE KEON

One afternoon not long ago the Toronto Maple Leafs were going through the paces of a strenuous practice when their ex-captain, George Armstrong, pointed to number 14 on the ice. "If that guy with the hair ever learns to skate," said Armstrong, "I think he'll do all right in this league."

This, of course, was Armstrong's idea of a joke because number 14 just happened to be his successor as Leaf captain, Dave Keon, who just happens to be about the fastest skater this side of the Olympics.

Formerly known for his close-cropped brush-cut, captain Keon now sports a mod, bushy mane. But in this, his 10th season in the National Hockey League, Dave appears none the slower for it; nor was he any slouch in the Leaf's losing cause last season.

Although the Toronto sextet had less than a successful campaign it was no fault of Keon's. Dave scored a very respectable 32 goals and 30 assists, for 62 points. What's more, he made it abundantly clear that he was an excellent choice to step into Armstrong's vacated captain's chair.

This really shouldn't have surprised anybody because in his own quiet way Keon always betrayed the signs of leadership. The problem has been that he has a choir boy's look and a "sotto voce" manner. But just give him the opportunity and he'll show anyone what leadership is all about.

Keon, all 5-9, 163 pounds of him, has been more or less in charge of the Toronto Maple Leafs for the past few years and, more or less, has been doing a creditable job.

Keon, perfectionist that he is, may not agree with that. He'll point out that a few seasons ago he came up with only 11 goals and 37 assists. "Regardless of all the contributions you make to a team," he pointed out, "you still like to score. Obviously I was disappointed with eleven goals."

There were those who suggested that time and new collection of brawnier hockey players finally caught up with the Lilliputian Leaf center. It was hinted that maybe they were pushing Keon into more and more corners and battering his somewhat frail physique more than it could rightfully absorb. It was enough to make one wonder whether Dave Keon was through as a very good hockey player.

Keon replied two seasons ago with 27 goals and 34 assists for 62 points, second highest on the Maple Leafs and a commendable figure from any point of view. He also led the Leafs in their brief playoff adventure with the Boston Bruins.

Last season under manager Jim Gregory and coach John McLellan, Keon became a new man in at least one way. Dave let his hair grow to near Beatle proportions, a factor that wouldn't have been possible under his former boss, general manager-coach George "Punch" Imlach. Under Imlach the Leaf morale deteriorated to a point of no return and there are people who believe that Keon suffered as much as anybody.

"When guys are down," he once observed, "maybe you've got to boost them. Keep hammering and you pound them down further. People forget that nobody starts out to play a bad season. You don't plan to look bad."

There was nothing slow about Keon's ascendancy into the Leafian hierarchy since he joined the club in 1960. He tasted Stanley Cup champagne four times and won the Calder Memorial Trophy as rookie of the year. He is a two-time winner of the Lady Byng Trophy for gentlemanly and effective play and also a two-time winner of the J. P. Bickell Cup as Leaf MVP. Four years ago he was voted the Conn Smythe Trophy as the most valuable player in the Stanley Cup playoffs.

"Dave's a leader," ex-Leaf trainer Bob Haggert pointed out. "He doesn't wait around for things to happen. He makes them happen."

Sometimes he finds himself in trouble, like the night he was in the middle of a major brawl between his teammates and the Rangers. Keon decided to play the mediator with somewhat dubious results.

"All I wanted to do," he explained, "was see that everything was even."

Despite Keon's well-heralded exploits over the years a considerable question remains in terms of his position in relation to the NHL's great centers.

"He is the best center in hockey," Maurice 'Rocket' Richard, the Montreal Canadiens' immortal scorer, said several years ago.

But since then Keon's star has fallen somewhat. His primary problem has been size. Speed has always been his forte, plus a fairly large repertoire of stickhandling. But Keon's problems developed in the hairy rink corners where the bruising defensemen would mow him down with elbows, knees and assorted other devices not calculated to help a little man.

His potential seemed to reach the apex about four years ago and since then he's shown nothing new in the way of moves to fool the opposition.

An example of Dave's problems cropped up early last

season when the Philadelphia Flyers, a nondescript Western Division team that normally would have been laughed out of Maple Leaf Gardens, skated into Toronto on October 22 and whipped the home club, 4-3.

Apart from the usual disgrace over losing to an expansion team the Leafs reeled from the fact that Keon's line was on the ice for three of Philadelphia's four goals. It was a time when Dave might have been the needed sparkplug but his help wasn't there. "We couldn't play that bad again if we tried," says Leaf coach John McLellan.

Well, that's as debatable as the future of the Leafs, which in turn is as debatable as Keon's future.

"Toronto's problem," says a Canadian journalist who followed the Leafs for more than a decade, "is it has too many small forwards."

The finger was pointing at the Keon line with Floyd Smith and Murray Oliver on the wings. Both Smith and Oliver, like their pivot, were minuscule types compared with the Walt Tkaczuks and Phil Espositos. In the significant loss to Philadelphia it was Keon's wings as much as anyone who put a burden on him.

"You could finger Floyd Smith on two goals," said Red Burnett, the veteran 'Toronto Daily Star' reporter, "and Murray Oliver on the other."

Size alone will never defeat a good hockey player. Henri Richard of the Canadiens who has been around as long as Keon, is built along the same minuscule lines, but appears to be headed for more of hockey because he plays an aggressive game.

"Richard," says one long time ice observer, "will fight back against the big men, but Keon will be content to bob and weave away from them. I can't blame Davey for that but the pugnaciousness of a Richard has a better psychological effect than a dodging Keon."

In its way the advantage of Richard over Keon is like Paul Newman in "Cool Hand Luke." Newman plays an affectionate but stubborn prisoner set upon by a fellow convict who towers over him in height and weight. The two battle and Newman obviously is the underdog. He is knocked down over and over again, yet keeps coming back for more until he is practically unconscious.

The bully finally clouts him a good one with such

finality it appears that Newman is dead. But, slowly and relentlessly, he regains his consciousness and then, to the bully's astonishment, he gets to his feet and actually flails away at the big guy. This so awes the bully that he quits the fight in disgust.

By the same token Richard's aggressiveness has the same drugging effect on his tormentors until they once and for all give up on the guy. Keon, by contrast, lacks that extra drive to keep the foes away and it appears his effectiveness is diminished by that very behavior.

The Leaf center appears to be relying more on his slapshot from distances farther away from the net, thus increasing his shots on goal figures but decreasing his scoring effectiveness. The long slap shots are for the most part easily turned away by enemy goalkeepers.

This is not to suggest that Dave Keon is washed up. There appears to be plenty of life in his lithe legs; he shows no inclination to toss in the skates.

What matters now is just how much he can help the Leafs rebuild from the ashes and whether he can lead the young Toronto players.

If he can do that, there's no question that Dave Keon has the right to be classified among the truly outstanding Leaf centers along with Syl Apps, Joe Primeau, Max Bentley and Ted Kennedy of bygone years.

FRANK MAHOVLICH

Tragedy is etched all over the whitish, high-browed face of Frank Mahovlich. The eyebrows turn sorrowfully down to his cheeks. The head tilts embarassedly to the side as if he were grieved to step on the ice and face 15,000 critics in Detroits Olympia Stadium.

The whole business of being the premier left wing on

the Red Wings is a challenge to 'The Big M' the way being prince of Denmark must have been for Hamlet.

He suffered two nervous breakdowns when he played in Toronto. His dispute with general manager-coach Punch Imlach was so severe that neither player nor boss exchanged a word for five years. His goal-scoring dropped from a high of 48 in 1961 to an abysmal 18 in 1967. "It reached a point," says Mahovlich, lightly creasing his brow in three places, "where I felt I was beating my head against a wall. If I had to play in Toronto one more year I'd probably retire, although I like hockey and wouldn't want to leave it."

As hockey players go, in March 1968 Mahovlich was like a beat-up Rolls-Royce. Whereas his long legs once blurred him from one end of the rink to another, he now appeared indolent and weak. His booming shot was virtually muted and he was regarded as a poor risk in the NHL's used-skater market.

On March 3rd, 1968, Sid Abel, the general manager of the Detroit Red Wings, decided to take that risk and obtained Mahovlich in a complicated seven player deal that was one of the biggest in hockey.

More important than that was the fact that the trade not only saved the hockey career of Frank Mahovlich, it turned him back into a superstar. It lured him out of his social coccoon and inspired a personality transformation that would make Jekyll and Hyde seem piddling by comparison.

"I said I'd be tickled if Frank scored 35 goals in his first year at Detroit," said ex-Red Wing coach Bill Gadsby. "Thirty wouldn't have been so bad either."

But the six-foot, 205 pound Mahovlich scored 49 goals, the most he's ever scored in 12 NHL seasons. It was the most goals for a Red Wing player since Gordie Howe scored the same number in 1952-53. No Detroit player ever scored more goals in a season. It also earned him a berth on the NHL's Second All-Star Team and he was voted the number one star of the 1969 All-Star Game in Montreal. And last year he had a commendable 38 goals and 32 assists, second best in Detroit.

"I've never seen Frank skate like he's skating here in Detroit," says teammate Bobby Baun, who played with

Mahovlich in Toronto. "I've never seen him so relaxed. Just getting out of Toronto has made a world of difference in him."

To Mahovlich Toronto represented one big haunted city. He was recognized and hounded wherever he went by fans who were never satisfied with his play. He clashed with teammates over his temporary refusal to join the Player's Association. And then there was the spectre of Imlach who bothered him more than all of the other things put together.

In Imlach's mind, Punch commanded with the authority of Napoleon, the wisdom of Socrates and the insight of Einstein. The violin-playing Leaf boss believed that all players, though constructed differently, should be treated equally. "Yeah," added one ex-Leaf, "equally bad."

When it came to Mahovlich, Imlach lost points immediately. Punch had an irritating propensity for mispronouncing his name MA-HAL-A-VICH instead of MA-HOV-LICH. Frank is a sensitive man who happens to be a connoisseur of champagne. He went to France in 1969 to bring back a few bottles of the very best *Moet et Chandon*. He would just as soon discuss scientific research on live chick as he would stick handling.

"Imlach refused to understand him," said Paul Rimstead, sports editor of *The Canadian Magazine*. "The relationship deteriorated to the point where Mahovlich no longer could play his best hockey for the Leafs."

It wasn't always that way. Punch and Frank were almost chummy from the time Mahovlich was rookie-of-the-year in 1957-58 until 1960-61 when The Big M scored 48 goals and was regarded as the Maple Leafs Most-Holy-Blessed-Be-He.

But to many observers the crack in their relationship first developed late in the 1960-61 season after Mahovlich addressed a banquet in London, Ontario. A day later Frank and his teammates were on a plane heading for a road game when The Big M picked up the morning paper. He fidgeted nervously as he read the headline and then proceeded down to the story.

The account asserted that Mahovlich told the banquet audience that teammate Red Kelly was not contributing *that* much to Frank's success. The Big M pulled himself together, walked over to Kelly and insisted he had been misquoted. Kelly was sympathetic and told Frank to forget the whole bloody thing.

Mahovlich then approached Imlach and pointed out that the story was all wrong. Imlach wasn't impressed; and that was the beginning of the end of the Mahovlich-Imlach love affair although it took several seasons before their divorce became irrevocable.

One day Frank analyzed the experience in the office of Jim Bishop, the Red Wings' executive director. He plunked himself in Bishop's swivel chair, removed his olive cap and leaned back with his hands folded behind his head. He was wearing a blue turtle-neck shirt with green stripes and black dungarees and appeared more relaxed than the men from Marlboro Country.

"I actually liked the guy (Imlach) for about five years," Mahovlich said, using his index finger to make a point. "Then things weren't the same after that. He just wasn't the guy I once knew. He started to do a lot of funny things; I told some of the guys on the Wings what he did and they refused to believe me. They gave me the double-look."

One of the favorite tortures in the Imlach concentration camp was inflicted after a losing weekend of hockey for the Leafs. They'd play at home on Saturday night and then travel as far as Chicago or Boston for a Sunday night game.

Frank scratched his left sideburn, which dropped halfway down the side of his ear. "We'd catch a plane back to Toronto on Monday morning and then he would take us directly from the airport to the rink for a practice. If that were the case, why didn't he practice us on the ice right after the game?

"After a while I began to wonder how long I could take this kind of thing. A day off from hockey does a man a lot of good but we never seemed to get a day off with Imlach."

Then there were the demands from the supposedly sophisticated Toronto fans. If Frank scored 48 goals when he was 23 years old, they reasoned, he should score at least 50 goals a year later. On top of that Chicago owner Jim Norris offered $1,000,000 for Mahovlich but the

Leafs turned him down. When Frank slipped to 33 goals in 1961-62 a few vocal purists in Maple Leaf Gardens began what was to be a chronic chorus of boos whenever The Big M played a mediocre game. Soon the hoots began grating his nerves, not to mention the feelings of other stars around the league.

"If Toronto fans would appreciate his great talent and give him the cheers he deserves instead of booing him, maybe the pressure wouldn't cook the guy," said Gordie Howe.

It was too late. Mahovlich couldn't conceal his anxiety. He became introverted and distant. "I played with him eleven years," said teammate Bob Baun, "and I didn't say twenty-two words to the guy."

Frank swung back and forth in the swivel chair, looking up at the ceiling and mulling over the tension-filled Toronto situation. Then he braked the chair, stopped, leaned forward as the insight flashed. "We had one roommate all year in Toronto. Here, they alternate roommates; you get to know all the guys. There was tension in Toronto. I wasn't the only one to feel it, and I think some of the other players reflected it too. One year Mike Walton walked out on the team. You talk to a lot of guys who were traded from Toronto and you find they don't feel too highly about Imlach."

In Toronto hockey is by far the number one sport. It is the only city that has three English-language dailies carrying by-lined stories about the Leafs every day from September through the end of the playoffs in April. He began to feel hounded by some of the reporters and burrowed even deeper into a shell. "When we were in Toronto," said teammate Pete Stemkowski, "you were lucky to get a hello from Frank."

Mahovlich succumbed to his first breakdown on November 12, 1964. He was suffering from what doctors later described as "deep depression and tension" but the exact diagnosis wasn't made public at the time. "We did not have Frank's permission," said Dr. Hugh Smythe, the Leafs' physician.

While Torontonians indulged in the usual wild speculation about The Big M's condition, Frank remained in seclusion for a couple of weeks before returning to the

Leaf lineup. He remained secretive about his ailment and also became exceptionally confidential about his interviews with reporters.

Once, a season later, Paul Rimstead asked to talk to him. "Okay," said Frank, "but not on the team bus. I'll see you later sometime."

They eventually held their rendezvous at a Montreal hotel where Mahovlich allowed that his relationship with Imlach was worsening. The Big M pointed out that his doctor advised him to ignore Punch whenever possible. "He told me to pull an imaginary curtain around myself whenever Punch was around," Frank said. "I've been doing it and I feel a lot better."

But there were other problems, other annoyances. Some hockey people close to the Leaf scene believe the team's policy toward endorsements helped turn off Mahovlich even more.

"Each Toronto player collected a flat $1,500 from Maple Leaf Sport Productions, the Leafs' company," said Al Eagleson, advisor to the Players' Association. "That hurt Mahovlich. There were years when he could have picked up $25,000 from endorsements. I had an offer of $5,000 from one firm for one season. He had to decline because of the Leaf commitment."

And the boos became more frequent and more annoying. In the middle of the 1967-68 season Mahovlich played superbly as the Leafs routed the Montreal Canadiens 5-0 at Maple Leaf Gardens. Frank scored a goal and two important assists and even his arch-critic, Imlach, described Frank's game as "outstanding."

He was named the second of three stars picked after every home game by broadcaster Foster Hewitt. Normally a "star" is greeted with cheers or, at worst, mild applause when he skates out on the ice to acknowledge the selection. When Frank planted his blades on the ice he heard some applause; but there also was no mistaking the boos that clearly represented a vocal minority.

Mahovlich completed the ritual and returned to the dressing room. He showered and changed into civilian clothes and later headed for the team's sleeping car which would carry the Leafs to Detroit for their next game. The Big M boarded the sleeper and prepared to go to bed.

But, somehow, he couldn't shake the memory of the catcalls and he couldn't get himself to sleep.

Torn by his anxiety Mahovlich finally walked off the sleeper at about 4 a.m. He contacted a club doctor and was escorted to a hospital. This time it was no secret. Dr. Hugh Smythe disclosed that The Big M was suffering from "deep depression and tension" and was in the care of Dr. Allen Walters, a psychiatrist.

"The barbs hurt him," said *Toronto Daily Star* sports editor Milt Dunnell. "Many players could shake it off but Mahovlich never was able to do it. He retreated within himself. The club officials have to ask themselves whether a person of The Big M's temperament ever can attune himself to the animosity of their sport—the animosity which he hears—not the violence which he feels on the ice."

The Maple Leaf brass had begun thinking about dealing Frank to another team but they couldn't make a move until he returned to the lineup and proved to the satisfaction of prospective buyers that he was capable of playing big-league hockey again.

His sabbatical proved beneficial to both Mahovlich and the Leafs, and he once again rejoined the club after a few week's rest. Recalling his mood at the time, Frank leaned forward on the reclining chair and placed his hands on Bishop's desk.

"It was getting pretty bad," he said. "By this time I hadn't talked to him (Imlach) for five years. I would have liked to talk to somebody about it but the way the Leaf setup worked, Imlach was boss of everything so I couldn't talk to anybody."

Early in March 1968 Imlach finally concluded a deal with Abel. The Leafs would receive Norm Ullman, Floyd Smith and Paul Henderson in return for Mahovlich, Pete Stemkowski and Garry Unger, all forwards.

In addition the Leafs would receive the rights to obtain ace defenseman Carl Brewer who had quit pro hockey but might be induced to return.

The deal was one of the most spectacular ever negotiated in the NHL. Ullman, an efficient center, was the ninth highest goal-scorer in league history. Henderson was a very promising young scorer while Smith was a journeyman with a knack for scoring goals. In addition to Mahovlich the Leafs lost Stemkowski, a hard-checking center, and Unger, a rookie with great potential.

Mahovlich, of course, was delighted to be free of Imlach's shackles. For years the Red Wings were renowned as a relaxed team with an obvious "joie de vivre." During playoff time manager Abel would take his men to the race track rather than seclude them in some distant hideaway. Frank was aware of this but he wasn't quite sure about how the Detroit players would react to him.

"There was pressure at first," he recalled. "Some of them heard the Frank Mahovlich stories and they were wondering if they were true. And I was never the kind of guy who tried to sell myself."

Gradually, both players and newsmen began to notice the metamorphosis. The Big M began to laugh and joke with his cronies and, pretty soon, he became one of the boys. "I really feel bad that I didn't take the time or make the effort to get to know him in Toronto," said Baun.

His 49 goal total in 1968-69 was the most ever scored by a Red Wing left winger. He led the team in three-star votes and scored the goal that resulted in Gordie Howe's 1,000th assist.

With 118 goals the Howe-Mahovlich-Delvecchio line had broken the 105-goal record set in 1943-44 by the famed Punch Line of Maurice Richard, Toe Blake and Elmer Lach. Its 264 points smashed the 223-point mark set in 1956-57 by Detroit's Production Line of Howe, Lindsay and Ullman. The line, incidentally, out-goaled 118-110 Boston's crack line of Phil Esposito, Ken Hodge and Ron Murphy although Esposito finished the 1968-69 season with a record-breaking 126 points.

For Howe it was a special treat because Mahovlich was the finest left wing he had the pleasure of working with since Hall of Famer Ted Lindsay quit hockey. It also was tribute to Howe's versatility that he could mesh so easily with such different stylists as Lindsay and Mahovlich.

"I can't figure two guys being any more different," said Howe. "Ted was rambunctious. He'd lay the lumber on everybody. Frank skates for those holes. I've never seen a player who could skate for those holes better than Frank. Ted was quick like a quarter-horse. From the net to the blue line he'd beat Frank in a race. But from the net to the far blueline Frank could beat Ted. Frank is fast.

"Ted had stamina but Frank has strength. Frank rushes down the ice a couple of times and then he must head for the bench to get some wind. Ted could do it maybe four, five or six times before he needed to collect wind. Frank can skate right over people, but he doesn't have the stamina for a big guy that Ted had.

"You have to lead Frank pretty good with a pass. Ted could take a pass in his skates or behind him or wherever it happened to be. Frank is a positional player. Ted wasn't. He was a darter. Frank is easier to play with in that way because you know where he'll be."

More than anyone, Howe made The Big M feel at home in Detroit. "He wouldn't let me be a loner," said Frank, propping his shoes against a trash can. "When I knew him as an opponent he seemed to me to be a tough guy, a dirty type player. Now I see him in a different light. He has a lot of feeling for everyone on the team. He's a very understanding guy."

Perhaps the greatest tribute—and most threatening from Frank's viewpoint—was delivered by Imlach who secretly contacted Abel in the middle of the 1968-69 season and attempted to return Mahovlich to the Leafs.

"I made a pass at Mahovlich," Imlach admitted. "I needed a left winger and Mahovlich was the only Detroit left winger I'd consider. I offered Abel a two-for-one trade and he said he wasn't interested in parting with The Big M. But I wouldn't say I made a mistake in trading him. I'd still make that deal over again. We got a great player in Ullman."

Imlach, of course, was wrong.

Ullman and Henderson played poorly for the Leafs in 1969-70 and Floyd Smith was virtually anonymous. Meanwhile, Mahovlich, Unger, Brewer and Stemkowski starred for Detroit, leading them into a playoff berth. The Leafs which Imlach had left in ruins for John McLellan finished a dead last.

Mahovlich is delighted he's in Detroit and wishes Imlach well now that Punch is running the new Buffalo Sabres.

"The years are gone," he said somberly. "What's done is

done. But when I think back and see that they fired Imlach in 1969 I find it hard to believe. I mean why didn't they fire him five years earlier when he started all the crap?"

This observer knew what Frank was thinking but he felt obliged to answer the question. "I guess Punch was winning at the time."

He digested the answer. He thought about all the years when Toronto should have been on top and just barely squeezed into the playoffs and he thought about the painful years behind him.

"You say he won," he said reflectively. "Well, Hitler won, right? The question you have to wonder about is—what is winning?"

STAN MIKITA

When life was at its bleakest for the Chicago Black Hawks in October 1969 the performance of one—and only one—player would determine whether the Hawks would climb out of the well. That was Stan Mikita.

At the time Bobby Hull was a holdout and the Hawks were loaded with rookies. The management was committed to a totally new defense-oriented system that was not exactly part of Mikita's bag. Chicago lost its first five games and Black Hawk fans began singing "Goodbye Billy" (Reay) as a lament to the beleaguered coach.

But Mikita never wavered in his desire to lift the Black Hawks and, slowly but surely, the rookies began to jell and the tables turned. Nobody had more reason to complain at the time than the 30-year-old center, Mikita. His pal and longtime linemate, Ken Wharram, had been hospitalized by a heart attack. His other linemate, Doug Mohns, was transferred to defense and Stan was compelled to launch the critical campaign on a line with Dennis Hull, Bobby's kid brother, and rookie Cliff Koroll.

With Bobby Hull out of the lineup, Wharram in the hospital and the Hawks using an uncertain goalie, Tony Esposito, it was essential that leadership be provided. Mikita came through. "He's just about the proudest and most dedicated player I've seen in 30 years of being around hockey players," says coach Billy Reay. "There isn't a player who works harder for himself or for his team than Stan."

Even after Bobby Hull returned it was Mikita who provided the offensive spark. The Chicago sextet was soon recognized as not merely a playoff team but one that could make serious race for The Prince of Wales Trophy. Unfortunately for Mikita, the new accent on defense and a few old grudges militated against him when it came time for selection to the mid-season All-Star Team.

Mikita was overlooked by newspapermen who pick the team but he could have been added to the squad by Montreal coach Claude Ruel who had the option to add players. "I suspect there was some politics there," said Mikita.

Whether he made the All-Stars or not was irrelevant. Stan spearheaded the Hawks to their stunning—and first time ever in league history—climb from last place to first this year. In the process he made a first-class hockey player out of Koroll. "I can't think of a better way to break into the NHL than as a wing for Mikita," the rookie explained. "All I have to do is keep my stick on the ice and watch what he does. He shows you something new every game."

Stan finished the season in third place on the scoring list with 39 goals, 47 assists and 86 points. His 50 minutes in penalties indicated he was not of Lady Byng Trophy calibre anymore but not overly tough either. But the inner toughness is there and it can be manifest many ways like the time he was freely sampling after shave lotions in a Montreal hotel.

A saleslady noticed the exhibition and dashed over to Mikita and admonished him with a "What do you think you're doing?" The Chicago ace and only NHL Triple Crown-winner explained that he was merely testing the product. The lady reacted as if he were chipping the Hope Diamond.

"You tried it," she said, "now you have to buy it."

Mikita smiled. "What do you mean? If I go into a shoe store and I try on a pair of shoes it doesn't mean I have to buy them, does it? I got you that time, didn't I?" Then he turned and walked out.

The anecdote is significant in its symbolism—trouble and Mikita are usually not far apart. Even when he was winning the Lady Byng Trophy, finishing first in scoring and capturing the Hart Trophy, the Czech-born scorer was in the midst of controversy. Like the time people were talking about his decision to wear a helmet; or his battle with management over a better contract or his penchant for speaking out on just about any topic you name.

This is chronic Mikita and it was never more evident than at the NHL draft meetings in Montreal in June 1969 when most of the players acted like they were doing imitations of the sphinx at Ghiza. "Mikita," observed Red Burnett of the *Toronto Daily Star*, "was like a breath of fresh air on a hot sultry night. He was the only man willing to air a personal beef."

Resplendent in a mustache and goatee, Mikita was challenging the NHL rulemakers who trimmed the curved stick back from 1½ inches to one inch. This was a very significant bit of legislation considering that Mikita was the arch-designer of the curved blade and the man who orchestrates the puck with it the way Leonard Bernstein used to conduct the New York Philharmonic.

"It's a mistake what they've done," said Mikita. "They're trying to sell hockey on national television in the United States and instead of improving the show they're trying to kill one of its most exciting features.

"Look at the record—since the advent of the curved blade players are shooting more often and the shots are faster and more exciting. If they're going to trim it to one inch why don't they just take the curved stick away from us and be done with it?"

It's not likely, however, that the league moguls will tamper with Mikita's other creation, a helmet that not only protects the top of the player's head but also the portion around the ear. Stan developed it after a shot by teammate Doug Mohns nearly cost him his right ear.

The way Mikita designed it, the cup of an athletic supporter was attached to the hard hat and covered the tender portion of the ear. Opponents needled him suitably but Stan was impervious to the carping because he knew he had a good thing going. "An engineer worked with me and we kept making improvements," Mikita revealed. "We came up with a suspension kind of thing. The helmet is suspended just above the head but never touches it."

Mikita isn't theorizing. He was the guinea pig on the experiment and lived to tell the tale after crashing head-first into a goalpost at The Forum in Montreal. "Without the helmet," he said, "I'd have had a fractured skull. With the helmet I had a slight headache."

For the past few seasons Mikita has been giving opposing goaltenders a large headache what with his dancing shots, tantalizing stickhandling and general rink savoir faire. A onetime troublemaker, Stan curbed his penchant for penalties so remarkably he won the good conduct award twice in a row, but failed in his bid for a third straight Byng in 1968-69. Just about everyone on the continent saw him lose it one Sunday afternoon that winter when he fought with Boston's Don Awrey in a match that was carried on national television.

"I found that in the first part of the season I wasn't thinking much about a third straight Byng," Stan explained, "but in the second half I guess there was a tendency to dodge penalties. You'd have a chance to step into somebody and you'd have the thought 'there goes the old trophy.' "

Some Mikita-watchers contend that his non-belligerency tended to diminish his effectiveness as a scorer, but he has the facts to prove otherwise. "Just look at the book," he counters. "I won the scoring title twice when I won the Lady Byng. And I won it twice when I had around 150 minutes in penalties."

His 39 goals last season fell only one short of his all-time high of 40 set in 1967-68. There is little doubt that he could have reached at least 45 were he not hampered by a troublesome back that compelled him to wear a protective brace during every game. He did little complaining; which is typical of Stan. Mostly, he went out and inspired the Black Hawks when they needed it most.

"Hockey," he explains, "is a team game and every player has to make a contribution."

It's just that Mikita's happens to be bigger than the others'.

BOBBY ORR

In the midst of the 1970 Stanley Cup playoffs a couple of Boston newspapermen were complaining about how Bobby Orr had made life so difficult for them. "How many different ways can you describe his greatness?" said one of them, speaking for the rest of the media.

The fact of the matter is that the 22-year-old Bruins ace long ago exhausted the adjective machine. He revolutionized the game of hockey by becoming the first defenseman in history to lead the NHL in scoring and he dominates the game more than any other skater. That includes Gordie Howe, Bobby Hull and Jean Beliveau.

"No defenseman in the NHL," says Jerry Nason of the Boston Globe, "does so many things so well."

In 76 games Orr scored 33 goals and 87 assists for 120 points, a good 21 more than his nearest scoring rival, teammate Phil Esposito of the Bruins. What makes the accomplishment so mind-boggling is that Orr did it at an age when young men are just breaking into the league. Even more awesome is the inevitable fact that Orr will get better with each season.

"There's no reason why Bobby Orr should stand still," says Weston Adams, Sr., the Bruins' board chairman. "He can hone and polish his game. Just the experience he will keep on gaining in competition will improve him. Orr's game will mature as he matures."

To get a perspective on Orr all one has to do is flash

back to the Rangers-Bruins playoff series last April. Practically single-handed Orr demolished the Rangers with his defensive genius, not to mention seven goals which set a new league record for defensemen. Not surprisingly he became the first player in the NHL to win four awards. Orr was named First All-Star; captured the Norris Trophy as best defenseman and the Hart Trophy as the most valuable player and also was presented with the Conn Smythe Trophy as the best player in The Stanley Cup playoffs.

"He controls the whole game," said crack defenseman Brad Park of the Rangers. "He slows it down, then he speeds it up. He calms down their other defensemen, and without him their forwards wouldn't get nearly so many goals."

New York's general manager-coach Emile Francis put it another way: "He's the first one up the ice and the first one back."

"Every time you get something going," said Ranger goalie Ed Giacomin, "he seems to be there. It seems that every time I'm out on the ice, he's out there, too."

There are those who contend that Orr has not yet received sufficient praise from the league. Perhaps the league should strike a Bobby Orr Trophy right here and now for the young man. "He is unreal," says ex-Boston coach Harry Sinden. "He had the greatest season any professional athlete ever had."

Although he's a defenseman, Bobby can't contain himself. Since he's one of the best skaters in the National Hockey League and has one of the hardest shots he also plays the part of a forward and scores goals. This causes enormous confusion among writers and coaches who are required to select players for the All-Star Team. It is impossible to pick Bobby as the All-Star goalie *and* All-Star defenseman *and* All-Star right wing, left wing and center. As a result he was merely selected as first defenseman on the All-Star Team and also was voted the James Norris Trophy as the premier defenseman in hockey. It sounds redundant, of course, but so does anything said about Bobby Orr, the player. And, remember, he was a star at the age of 18 when he played his first major league game as a professional and has been getting better ever since.

Until Bobby Orr came along, nobody, but nobody in professional hockey—and that includes the super-dupers like Gordie Howe and Bobby Hull—earned more than $40,000. In the summer of 1968 Bobby Orr signed a three-year contract reportedly amounting to *$400,000*.

The exact figure of Orr's contract is not especially important. What matters is that this kid, even while he was still in his teens, was teaching hockey's supposedly sophisticated old pros what life was all about; and one of the first lessons is that you get paid the kind of bread you deserve. What Bobby Orr did that neither Mantle nor Lombardi nor Chamberlain did was lead the way toward the organization of a hockey player's union which has since lifted salaries to such a point, the average skater received $18,000 annually. Before Orr came along, the average was about $11,000.

Hockey's labor revolution erupted three years ago when it came time for the Bruins to sign the then 18-year-old Orr to a contract. Every 18-year-old who ever joined the National Hockey League had been delighted to sign for the salary offered by management.

The difference between Bobby and the other 18-year-olds was that he had an old friend named R. Alan Eagleson, who also happened to be a lawyer with a keen interest in hockey. Eagleson agreed to advise Orr in his negotiations and without so much as drawing a deep breath won a two-year, $75,000 contract. When veterans twice as old as Bobby got wind of the windfall they phoned Eagleson and requested his advice. It didn't take long before the National Hockey League Players Association was organized and players who once might have been jealous of Bobby, the prodigy, now were eulogizing him.

It is one thing to be a gifted athlete, which Bobby obviously is. It is another to be a wealthy athlete, which also is the case; but it's something else when you're gifted and wealthy and as perfectly wonderful as the fictitious "boy-next-door." Yet Bobby is just that and people who have been around enough to be super-cynics waste no time admitting it.

In the big-league hockey jungle, hard-bitten veterans go

(Black Hawks—Canadiens) Montreal: Chicago Black Hawks' goalie Tony Esposito, who recorded his first shutout of the National Hockey League season on October 25, 1969, gets set for one of the thirty shots the Canadiens rained in on him, this time one by Montreal's Ralph Backstrom (6) as Chicago's Pat Stapleton (12) belly-flops on the ice, in the second period. The Chicago Black Hawks won 5–0.   *(UPI)*

(Bruins—Canadiens) Montreal: Montreal Canadiens' John Ferguson watches Boston Bruin goalie Ed Johnston (mask) fail to save a shot on goal by Montreal's Ralph Backstrom on which Ferguson assisted. Bobby Orr (L) checks Ferguson while Dallas Smith (20) looks on. Montreal won the game played November 1, 1969, by a 9–2 score.   *(UPI)*

(BRUINS—BLUES) Boston: Where does one start seems to be the dilemma Linesman Pat Shelter (C) and Matt Pavelich (R) are faced with during first period battle between players at Boston Garden, November 5, 1969. Couples are (L, fore) Blues' Bob Plager and (L) Bruins' Ron Murphy; (L, rear) Phil Esposito and (L) Blues' Ron Anderson; and the ones that started it all (R, fore) Blues' Noel Picard and (rear) Bruins' Ken Hodge.   *(UPI)*

Tony Esposito in action against Oakland on November 15, 1969.
(UPI)

(BRUINS—BLUES) St. Louis: The Blues' Phil Goyette (hidden) is shoved from behind by Boston Bruins' Bobby Orr (4) as Goyette fought for loose puck near the Boston goal in second period of Boston—St. Louis game on December 18, 1969. Boston's Don Awrey (26) went down in the action as goalie Gerry Cheevers (30) reaches to try to knock puck away.   *(UPI)*

Tony Esposito makes a save on his brother Phil Esposito (7).
(UPI)

(WINGS—LEAFS) Detroit: Toronto goalie Bruce Gamble (30) stops a shot by Red Wing Gordie Howe (9) during the first period of the Detroit—Toronto game at Detroit's Olympia Stadium on December 21, 1969. Toronto won the game 3–0. *(UPI)*

St. Louis: Hockey greats, (L-R) Phil Esposito, Boston; Bobby Orr, Boston; Gordie Howe, Detroit, and Bobby Hull, Chicago, share a joke at the 23rd annual All-Star banquet on January 19, 1970. Phil Esposito received the Hart Memorial award for the most valuable player and the Art Ross trophy for most points. Bobby Orr received the James Norris Trophy for the outstanding defenseman for 1968—69 season. *(UPI)*

(NHL ALL-STAR) St. Louis: Autographing sticks for fans. All-Star stars for the East Division, Bobby Hull (L) and Gordie Howe (R) each scored a goal in the NHL All-Star game on January 20, 1970. The two old pros led the East to a 4—1 victory over the West Division in the 23rd annual All-Star game. *(UPI)*

(WINGS—HAWKS) Detroit: Chicago's Bobby Hull (9) is dumped by Detroit's Ron Harris during the first period of the Red Wings—Black Hawks game on January 22, 1970. Hull was bringing the puck over the red line when Harris caught him with a solid body check. Red Wing Gordie Howe (right) goes after the puck. *(UPI)*

Bobby Orr (4) in action against Detroit.   *(UPI)*

Boston: The National Hockey League (NHL) got around to pass-
ing out three of its top individual trophies for the 1968—69 seasons on January 25, 1970, when it honored Bruins' Phil Esposito
(L) and Bobby Orr (R) in the ceremonies at Boston Garden. NHL
President Clarence Campbell (C) presented Orr with the Norris
trophy as the league's outstanding defenseman and awarded both
the Art Ross Scoring Trophy and The Hart Most Valuable Player
award to Esposito.   *(UPI)*

(BRUINS–RANGERS) Boston: John McKenzie (19) of the Bruins pushes Rangers' Walt Tkaczuk's head back during a fight which erupted during second period action on April 8, 1970, at Boston Garden, as linesman Ron Ego skates up to the battling pair along with Bruins' Rick Smith. The Bruins won the game 8–2. *(UPI)*

(WINGS–HAWKS) Detroit: Black Hawk star Bobby Hull is dumped in front of the Detroit nets by Red Wing Bob Baun (4) during the second period of the Detroit–Chicago game April 12, 1970. Red Wing goalie is Roger Crozier, Chicago won, 4–2, to eliminate Detroit from Stanley Cup play. *(UPI)*

Boston: Blood spills frm the head of Rangers' Jean Ratelle (19) who kneels on the ice April 14, 1970, at the Boston Garden. Phil Esposito (front) received a five minute major penalty for slashing Ratelle in the second period of NHL quarter final playoff game for the Stanley Cup. Ranger goalie Ed Giacomin (1) skates to Ratelle's aid as Bruin Wayne Cashman (back) looks on. Bruins won the game 3–2. *(UPI)*

out of their way to "test" rookies. They'll thrust the point of their stick-blade in the stomach or they'll ram an elbow into the jaw. If the rookie doesn't hit back he's through. In a matter of months he'll be run right out of the league. When a rookie happens to be outdrawing a low-salaried veteran by two-to-one the "test" becomes even more severe.

One of Bobby's earlier tests was given by Ted Harris, a big, rawboned defenseman then with the Montreal Canadiens. Even under the most pleasant circumstances, Harris is mean and on this night he directed some of his venom at Bobby. There were no second thoughts. The kid dropped his stick, then his gloves, and tore at Harris. The Montreal bully went down; but he was up again and, then, down a second time. Orr had "won his spurs," and Bobby hasn't backed down since.

Opponents see all things in Orr but the best of them all, Gordie Howe, believes the essence of Bobby's superiority is his leg strength.

"He's got the legs," Howe explained. "He's also got a good attitude, plenty of desire and he always hustles. He's also an awfully nice kid. In the summer of 1968 I had my two boys with me on a promotional trip to Bobby's hometown, Parry Sound, Ontario, and Bobby was dressed in a white shirt and tie. As soon as the festivities were over we went to his house and he changed into a sweatshirt.

"It was the one which had a Gordie Howe crest on the front. My boys liked that."

Unconsciously Bobby's favorite word is "super." This is perfectly natural in view of his hockey-playing efforts. "Orr," says New York Post columnist Larry Merchant, "is at least hockey's sixth dimension. He is one of those rare athletes who revolutionizes his game as Babe Ruth did, as Bill Russell did. Bobby Jones once said of Jack Nicklaus, 'He plays a game with which I am not familiar.' Orr plays hockey in a way that makes old-timers feel like dinosaurs, too."

BRAD PARK

Late in March 1970, when it appeared that the New York Rangers were about to fall right out of a playoff berth, a young man with a cherubic face and a sinister—on ice—disposition returned to the lineup and at least temporarily rescued them from oblivion.

Brad Park had been deactivated for more than a month with a broken ankle and supposedly was lost to the Rangers for the rest of the season. But somehow he managed to climb back into his skates on March 25th and sparked the Rangers to a come-from-behind, 1-1, tie with the Montreal Canadiens that staved off New York's elimination. A night later Brad scored a power-play goal that orbited the Rangers to a 4-1 victory over Montreal and once more Park received a standing ovation from the Madison Square Garden audience.

"That kid is to our club what Bobby Orr is to the Bruins," said Ranger general manager-coach Emile Francis. "He makes things go out there. He can change the tempo of the game; and he is aggressive." Park, incidentally, was runner-up to Orr in voting for the Norris Trophy as the NHL's best defenseman.

Hard statistics underline Park's significance to the Rangers. He was absent from the lineup for 16 games and during that time the Rangers won three, lost ten and tied three. In the process they plummeted from first to fifth place in the East Division. Thus, it hardly was surprising that Park was named to the first All-Star Team.

"Brad's presence on the ice does something for the rest of the guys," said New York goalie Ed Giacomin.

Park's arrival in New York by no coincidence delivered a long-missing aura of respectability to the Ranger defense and set people to recalling what life had been like on the New York backline in bygone years.

About a decade ago when Douglas Bradford Park still was skating on his ankles on a playground rink in Toronto, the Rangers were playing the Red Wings at the old Madison Square Garden. It was a very significant game because Gordie Howe got mad at Lou Fontinato of the Rangers and nearly sliced Fontinato's ear off with the blade of his stick. That had never happened to a Ranger before.

Fontinato eventually had his ear restored to its proper place and since he was regarded as the best fighter in the National Hockey League, he eventually chased down Howe and attempted to beat him up. When Howe got through with him, Fontinato's nose looked like a one-way street sign bent in the middle at a 90-degree angle.

From that day on opponents regarded Howe with such respect he skated around the rink with an impunity that suggested an antique protected by an invisible shield. Dare touch that prize and a thousand alarms go off; you'd think you just stepped on a third rail.

As a worldly rookie at 20 years of age, Brad Park had a working knowledge of Howe's surgical capabilities when the rangers visited Detroit for a game late in 1968-69. He also knew that most young players got a solid case of lockjaw when they came up against Howe, who is not only hockey's Most-Holy-Blessed-Be-He but also one of the roughest players ever to lace on a pair of skates.

Park was singularly unimpressed. He was so unimpressed, in fact, that when The Great One lumbered in on the Ranger goal Brad crouched low and crunched his six-feet and 190 pounds into Howe's gut. "I was told to go low on the man," Brad recalls, "because if I went high I might get the stick in the mouth."

So far, so good. But what they forgot to tell the lad who looks like Buster Brown playing Edward G. Robinson is that Howe does not respect a clean bodycheck—when *HE* is a victim.

As Brad watched the puck move out of his zone he failed to notice Howe rise and skate back into the play. The next thing he *DID* notice was trainer Frank Paice standing over him with a vial of smelling salts. "He (Howe) got me in the neck. Pfwoop! Like that, with his stick."

Park, who looks like a slimmed-down butterball, clambered to his skates. Like all rookies who tried to mess with the Great God Howe before, Brad learned his lesson and that would be the end of it between he and Gordie.

Wait! What's this? Park skated over to Howe. Has he apologized?

"One more move like that," said Brad, his index finger directed at the mid-point between Howe's eyes, "and this stick goes down your throat."

As far as can be determined Howe has yet to make that move. But Brad has not forgotten. "I am," he says, "waiting for my chance."

To Howe and other victims around the NHL, Park is an impudent tough with a lot of ability. He has brazenly destroyed several Ranger rules of pacifism while cultivating a new form of Seventh Avenue ice militarism.

In the old, pre-Park days when a bully like Ted Green would beat up an innocent Ranger like Dave Balon, the New York players would stand around like helpless United Nations observers. Brad changed that in April 1969 during the Ranger-Canadiens Stanley Cup round. John Ferguson of the Canadiens, generally regarded as the heavyweight champion of hockey, was belaboring New York defenseman Jim Neilson with a flurry of lefts and rights. Park charged in and hauled Ferguson away. Unfortunately Brad neglected to notice Ted Harris, who rushed in and put a hammerlock around Park's neck.

"I have a pretty good memory," says Park, smiling so that you can easily see his half-broken upper tooth just off the center of his mouth. Better than his memory is his wit which is sprinkled laconically through any post-game conversation with the ease of a Woody Allen.

He demonstrated this early last season when that "Filthy McNasty" Ted Harris jumped Brad's former roommate, Bill Fairbairn, mounted him like a steer and proceeded to tar and feather the helpless Ranger.

Shazam!

Brad dropped his glove. He dropped his stick and dove headlong onto Harris, knocking him off Fairbairn. After that, as Park tells it, the contest was over. "I hit him a couple on the head," he laughs, squinting through his brown eyes, "then a couple on the chest. And then I proceeded to get mad."

A couple of weeks later he spent a good part of the evening attempting to run St. Louis Blues ace Red Berenson into the Hudson River. This persuaded a reporter to inquire after the game why he would pick on an upstanding citizen like Berenson. "Simple," says Brad, "he kept going around me."

"But," the man persisted, "you look like you really hated him."

He returns a look of surprise. "Well, he *IS* the enemy."

An impudent tough isn't snobbish about his victims, and Brad certainly wasn't playing the prig when he challenged Yvan Cournoyer, a chunky little fellow who gave away about 15 pounds and a couple of inches.

Park opened with a right hook that looked good enough to end the bout but Cournoyer returned with a right cross that startled and amused the young Ranger. "I'd be very embarrassed in front of all those people if I didn't win the fight," he says. With the next punch Cournoyer was down —and out.

Park's paymaster, Rangers general manager-coach Emile Francis, endorses the lad's misanthropy. "That's the way it should be," says Francis who has seen Rangers drawn and quartered by the enemy for too many years, "and that's the way it has to be. I like when Brad jumps in."

He'd like it less if Park weren't among the top two of some 65 defensemen in the league. This in itself is a phenomena that neither Francis, nor his corps of scouts, nor just about anybody can figure out. How come this bumptious bumper got so far, so fast without anybody really knowing about him?

The answer, of course, is his impudence.

When he showed up at training camp in Kitchener, Ontario, in September 1968 with his mother and father he looked like the sports editor of a high school newspaper bent on a story about goalie Ed Giacomin. But he talked with the mustard tongue of a Derek Sanderson. We all laughed at him. He was a nice kid who was about tenth in line for the defense that had room for five, but he seemed to have delusions of grandeur above and beyond the call of duty.

"I'm shooting for the third spot on defense," Brad offhandedly mentioned to me and Carl Martin of the *Hudson Dispatch*. "That way the worse that'll happen is I'll wind up fifth man."

Martin is a reasonable fellow. He asked me if he had heard the kid right. I asked him the same question. We agreed that Park was putting us both on.

Then we saw him play.

It was no put-on.

He was so good he complicated Francis' life. The boss wanted Al Hamilton to round out the defense with veterans Harry Howell, Jim Neilson, Arnie Brown and Rod Seiling. Hamilton was heir apparent, having labored in the minor leagues for a couple of years waiting for this opening.

Francis fulfilled his obligation to Hamilton but he had a bigger obligation to the team. And when it became obvious that Park was orchestrating every game he played for Buffalo in the American League there was no choice but to drop Hamilton and elevate Park. Which he did.

Within a month Park demonstrated the puck-carrying ability of perennial All-Star Doug Harvey, the truculence of John Ferguson, the "cool" of Gordie Howe and that special quality of the great ones known in the trade as "hockey sense."

"He'll be around a long, long time," says Oakland Seals defenseman Harry Howell, who played in New York for 16 years. "It's very rare you see a young defenseman with so much poise."

Or so much humor.

The quips fly from his Henny Youngman lips as fast as the puck leaves his stick on a slapshot. When he collected four assists as the architect on four goals against the Pittsburgh Penguins in February 1969 an observer noticed he had yet to score a goal. And, the man wondered, how did Park plan to celebrate his first big-league goal?

Park replied immediately: "I'll give myself a standing ovation."

A few games later he scored his first NHL goal against the Boston Bruins. He put so much of himself into the shot that when the red light flashed Brad was incapable of giving himself *ANY* kind of ovation. He was face-down on the ice, looking very much like the seal act in Barnum & Bailey.

The 17,250 clients who regularly fill Madison Square Garden have their long-awaited defensive hero. "We Want Park" choruses echoed off the arena ceiling, and even so reserved a critic as Francis—who has to sign Park's contract—enthused. "Mister Park," said Francis, "is playing tremendously. You notice I call him *MISTER* Park."

When he was six years old and known as *MASTER* Park not Mister, Brad learned how to skate in a town called Unionville, a few miles out of Toronto. Hall of Famer Max Bentley gave him his first pair of skates at age four. He played goal in his first game and was beaten on the first shot so he sat down and cried.

His mother, Betty Park, who was a phys ed instructor in the Royal Canadian Air Force during World War II, watched the play and wondered what her son was bawling about. "He wasn't supposed to do that," Brad explained between his tears.

Betty and Bob Park guided their son through the Toronto sandlot hockey leagues with a mixture of diligence and delight. After each game father and son would huddle around the kitchen table to talk strategy. "They'd move the salt and pepper shakers around the table to illustrate a play," says Mrs. Park. "Then they'd go into the living room, push aside the sofa and chairs and take each other out of the play."

An overdose of parental interest could have ruined the kid but the Parks were intelligently candid in their approach. More important, they knew what they were talking about and Brad realized it.

"We are his two biggest fans," says Bob Park, "and his two sternest critics."

Mr. and Mrs. Park jetted to New York last season to watch the Rangers defeat the St. Louis Blues. An hour after the game Mrs. Park took her son aside and reminded him about the time Berenson and Frank St. Marseille nearly outwitted him on a two-on-one break. "Listen, Brad," said Betty, laying it on the line, "when you've got a guy like St. Marseille in your sights, for Heaven's sakes, let him have it!"

Bob Park, who coaches a peewee team in Toronto, chimed in, "The boy has got a helluva lot to learn. And I, for one, think he can get better, the way Bobby Orr can. But he's gone beyond the point where I can help him."

He's a sponge for learning and his teammates appreciate it. Right from the start goalie Ed Giacomin told him what he wanted from a defenseman and he's still telling him.

"The only thing wrong," says Gaicomin whose hair is grey because of it, "is that he tends to go too deep in the other end and sometimes gets caught up ice."

Originally he was teamed with Jim Neilson but early in 1969-70 Francis moved him on a line with Arnie Brown and switched Neilson over to Rod Seiling's unit. It was a difficult adjustment for a youngster like Park who had played only with Neilson since he came up but he made it without too much trouble.

"His advantage," says Neilson, "is that he's a real good skater. When you can maneuver fast, you recover from your mistakes."

A barometer of Park's significance in the NHL today is the fact that opponents are using him as a standard of comparison. "My guy, Keith Magnuson, is going to be a real good one," Chicago Black Hawks coach Bill Reay was saying recently of his rookie defenseman. "He's developing so fast; reminds me a lot of Brad Park."

"There is no question," says Detroit Red Wing ace Carl Brewer, after whom Park is compared, "that Brad is going to be among the great ones!"

DEREK SANDERSON

One afternoon in March 1970 WCBS-TV sportscaster Bill Mazer asked Derek Sanderson of the Boston Bruins whether he preferred to be known as a tough guy or a lover.

The Bruins' long-haired center mulled over the question for about a half-second and replied, "I'd rather be known as a hockey-player!"

Mazer wasn't exactly surprised at the response because Sanderson has become renowned as the most glib young man in the National Hockey League, as well as its most colorful dresser and, certainly, one of its most accomplished centers.

As hockey players go, Sanderson is a revolutionary in the best traditions of Thomas Paine and George Washington, with a touch of Nathan Hale thrown in for good measure. Derek might easily have paraphrased Hale when he said he had but one life to give for his Bruins, and he is in the process of giving them everything he has.

Bruins' board chairman Weston Adams, Sr., discovered Sanderson when Derek was a 15-year-old playing junior B hockey in Stamford, Ontario. "Right away I knew this was a player we'd want on our side someday," said Adams recently. "Sanderson is a great competitor. There are players in this league who can do this thing and that thing better than he does. But nobody, basically, is the competitor he is. Derek looks at hockey the same way I do. Once they drop that puck on the ice, he hates the hell out of the opposition."

He may hate the opposition but he certainly loves girls.

Girls come easy to Sanderson; as easy as they come to his buddy Joe Namath. He's six-feet tall and 176 pounds and damn good looking. After his appearance on Namath's television show the women temporarily forgot about Joe Willy and swarmed around Derek. He looked like a hip Clint Eastwood.

Girls come so easy to Derek he doesn't flip when they surround him. You might say he's a connoisseur of the species. "There are no better women in North America than in Montreal," he explains. "Pittsburgh is terrible. The good cities are Los Angeles, San Francisco, Boston, New York, Montreal and Toronto."

Up until last summer Sanderson admired Namath from afar. Then Derek's attorney, Bob Woolf, arranged a partnership in Namath's Boston edition of Bachelor's III and the pair have been swinging from bird to bird ever since.

"Joe Willy lined me up some dates in New York," Sanderson recently recalled. "They were great, man. He's good people, that Joe Willy. He's on to Playmate-of-the-Year stuff now."

Another of Sanderson's playmates is Ken Harrelson of the Cleveland Indians whom he also met through Woolf. Harrelson's influence can be reflected through Derek's main-floor bachelor apartment in suburban Brookline, Mass. The living room is a meadow of thick blue broadloom while the bedroom is carpeted in wall-to-wall white fur. At any given time there is a minimum of 45 suits in the pad. Needless to say, Derek does not lead a hermit's life at home.

"My kind of girl," he explains, "has to be feminine, but she has to have a head on her shoulders and know what she's doing. My whole theory is that a woman can interest you with her body but she can hold you with her mind. I like a girl who is really good looking, feminine, sensitive and soft. The type of girl who can fit into a dinner at the Waldorf or a draft beer down at the beach. Very few girls can do that. And she has to be a girl who can make a man feel like a man."

Some Sanderson-watchers are more awed by his appearance than his women. His long hair is so well-trimmed that Toronto columnist Dick Beddoes remarked, "You get the impression that if he combed it Namath would fall out."

Baltimore Clipper coach Rudy Migay added, "Is that Derek Sanderson or a Buffalo."

Last season the Bruins had a defenseman named Bill Speer, who was a barber by trade. Sanderson regarded Speer with mock fear. "I fended him off," said Sanderson. "I saved it for a hair-stylist in Boston. Margo, a good looking broad. Nothing serious. A sawbuck for a trim."

Sanderson remains candid about his looks. "If I were laying a price," Derek asserted, "I'd give odds that Rod Gilbert has the nicest hair in the league."

The Bruins' squarish general manager Milt Schmidt attempted to put the brakes on Sanderson's long hair and mod clothes but he might as well have built a bridge across the Atlantic for all the good it did. Soon, teammates Gerry Cheevers, Phil Esposito, John McKenzie and Bobby Orr followed suit.

"Orr used to have a brushcut," Derek recalls. "I told him 'Bobby, the brushcut, forget it'."

Nowadays, Orr's hair is worn neatly long. "I used to be pretty square," Orr admits, "and the worst thing I ever did to myself is wear a whiffle."

Derek is not unaware of his influence on NHL styles. "There are still a few bad dressers around," says Sanderson. "A few slow picker-uppers. But we're opening up the NHL's stuffed shirts."

One area in which Sanderson failed is in skates. He figured if Namath could wear white football shoes, he could wear white ice skates and he went about having a manufacturer design a pair for him.

"Sure he can wear white ice skates," said ex-Bruin coach Harry Sinden when he heard the news, "on the condition that he wears a pink helmet to go with it."

"The Bruins didn't see eye-to-eye with me on the white skates," Sanderson allows. "They're a little stuffy; they figure it's 'Americanizing' the game, and that the players who are nearly all Canadians might take offense. Milty (Schmidt) asked me not to wear them and I figure you can't change the system overnight."

That doesn't mean the white skates issue is a dead one. Far from it; but with Woolf's counseling Sanderson is learning to cut his revolutionizing speed a few knots.

"I'd like Derek to change the NHL in as graceful a way as possible," says Woolf, one of the country's foremost attorneys. "But I also want him to maintain a good relationship with management."

Actually, Sanderson's rapport with Schmidt is considerably better than it was with Milt's predecessor, Leighton "Hap" Emms. Not that that's very difficult. An old-line conservative, Emms was bounced from the Bruins when he antagonized Ted Green and Bobby Orr.

Sanderson's beef is legitimate. Emms signed him for coolie wages, and Derek won the Calder Trophy as rookie of the year in 1967-68. "The Bruins got me lousy cheap," he admits. "Ten grand for the first year, twelve grand the second year and a stinking thirteen last season."

Seasoned hockey men claim that in many ways Sanderson is the superior of high-scoring teammate Phil Esposito. He's genuinely tougher. He's better at face-offs—in fact, if Sinden had used Sanderson instead of Esposito on some key face-offs in the Montreal-Boston playoff series in the spring of 1969, the Bruins might have won the Stanley cup. Derek is also rated a better two-way player.

Before the 1969 East Division Cup final the Toronto *Daily Star* put two centers in perspective with a headline: "HABS FEAR SANDERSON MORE THAN ESPO."

The Canadiens recalled that Derek was the star in Boston's four-game sweep over Toronto. The Montreal forecast proved correct; Sanderson helped Boston to a 2-2 tie in games until a devastating check by John Ferguson disabled Derek for the remainder of the series.

It was no coincidence that the Bruins folded in six games. Sanderson condones Ferguson's check but frankly admits he's going to get even sooner or later. And when he says it, you better believe it!

"Sure I'm a dirty player," he admits. "I like playing dirty. Anyway, that's the way the game should be played. I like fighting. Maybe I'll get beat up a lot, but I'll get the guy eventually."

And he's gotten some good ones: Terry Harper, Ted Harris, Dick Duff and Orland Kurtenbach for starters. He rates Kurtenbach of Vancouver the best fighter in the league, and considers Gordie Howe one of the meanest players. He was warned to stay away from Howe but scoffs at the suggestion.

"One theory I go on," he says. "I don't care who he is, his face will bleed just like mine, right? That stick is a great equalizer. I've cut people so often I can't remember who or when. So has Howe."

Such irreverent pop-offs cause the Bruins' brass to shudder. Once when Derek delivered some choice remarks to Paul Rimstead, the former sports editor of 'The Canadian Magazine', coach Sinden snapped, "Is he shooting off his mouth again!"

Sinden can say what he pleases but Sanderson knows what he's after and he's getting the ink. During the non-hockey months he was a continual item in Boston papers, sometimes on the fashion page, sometimes on the society page and sometimes on the sports page. But always it was Sanderson.

"There are three things you need to make money in professional sports," he maintains, offering a superb clue to his philosophy. "One is talent. The second is points. The third is color. Orr has the talent. Esposito has the points. The only thing left for me is the color."

As a result you either dig Derek Sanderson a whole lot or you really put him down. And he *HAS* been put down.

Last season *Maclean's Magazine,* the national magazine of Canada, ran a profile on Sanderson. The mail response was one of the most emphatic the publication has received and many of the letters were classics of outrage.

"It's too bad you make a hero of a man not because of his prowess as a hockey player but because of his prowess with women, of his disregard for the rules of his profession and of his foppery in dress," wrote Douglas Brown of St. Martins, New Brunswick.

"Any professional hockey player who brags about his fights and his sex fun the night before a game is not much of an idol for young Canadians to worship," wrote V. Wightman of Bengough, Saskatchewan.

And so they raged into the night.

Derek isn't surprised. What revolutionary would be? But he won't stop there. Not on your life.

"I believe strongly in the hippie movement today," he says. "Everybody's groovin' and turning on. I know a lot of people who smoke pot (marijuana). Naturally in my position I can't stand that. Get caught once and that would be it. I don't approve of young kids smoking the stuff, but I don't condemn people for using it. It's not for me, though. But everywhere I go today, kids are givin' me the peace sign. It's groovy. There's nothing wrong with that—to turn on and stay on. That's exactly where it's at today."

Curiously enough, the Bruins management has been urging him to cut down on his chain-smoking of regular cigarettes. He agrees he should eliminate the habit, if possible.

"My theory is 'everything in moderation'," says Derek.

That's what the man said.

SERGE SAVARD

Early in March 1970 the Montreal Canadiens were playing the New York Rangers in a game the Flying Frenchmen just had to win if they were going to remain playoff contenders. The Rangers led the Canadiens by seven points and a victory for New York would virtually guarantee the Rangers a playoff berth and torpedo the Montrealers.

As it turned out the Canadiens won the game 5-3, and they were paced for most of the 60 minutes by a tall, husky French-Canadian named Serge Savard. "He's like two players," said Ranger general manager-coach Emile Francis. "He plays a solid defense and he can kill penalties with the best of them."

During one of his late tours of ice duty Savard made a desperate lunge to prevent a Ranger score and in the process fell heavily on his left leg, breaking it in two places. It was a blow that stunned the Montreal sextet. "I would rather have lost the two points," said Canadiens captain Jean Beliveau, "and have Serge back in the lineup."

But Beliveau's wish couldn't be granted because the talented Savard was through for the season. He would be unable to return for the hectic stretch run and Montreal missed the playoffs. It was a loss the Canadiens could ill afford to sustain because Savard, in the eyes of many, was the most valuable player on the team. He proved it in the spring of 1969 when he won the Conn Smythe Trophy as the best player in the Stanley Cup playoffs.

In describing Montreal's Stanley Cup champions not long ago Peter Gzowski, former editor-in-chief of Maclean's Magazine of Canada, pinpointed their distinct quality.

"On the ice," said Gzowski, "the Canadiens swoop and gambol, skating like fury and burning with zeal; they are somehow romantic, like Scaramouche or Cyrano or Jean Gascon."

It is an apt description. All we have to do is substitute a few names like Richard or Serge Savard.

The last one, Savard, of course is relatively new to the long and awesome Canadiens Hall of Stars, but there is strong evidence the 6-2, 200 pound defenseman will someday be compared with such honored Montreal backliners as Emile "Butch" Bouchard and Ken Reardon, not to mention the finest of them all, Doug Harvey.

Savard began assembling his credentials in the 1967-68 season, his rookie year. Montreal was up against St. Louis in the Stanley Cup finals. The Canadiens were leading the series 1-0 when the teams met for the second game on the Blues' home rink. A defeat for St. Louis would practically assure their burial.

The teams were tied, 0-0, as the clock ticked past the two minute mark of the third period. The puck dribbled into the corner of the rink not far from the Blues' net. Claude Provost of the Canadiens was the first to get there. He passed it out front as two Blues attempted to stymie him but they were a half-second too late.

There was an audible report as the six-ounce hunk of black vulcanized rubber cracked onto the stick of Serge Savard. It didn't stay there very long. Maybe two seconds. Then, whammo! Savard shot, and the puck sailed past goalie Glenn Hall. The time was 2:17 and neither team scored again. Montreal went on to the series and the Cup in four straight games.

It was a particularly gratifying goal for Savard. The St. Louis coach was Scotty Bowman, and if anyone had a score to settle with Bowman it was the young Montreal native.

"I played junior hockey for Scotty when he coached the young Canadiens in Montreal," Savard explained. "He used to have me take a cold shower before every game to make sure I was wide awake. Well, now you can tell Scotty I don't need a cold shower to wake up for this game."

If anyone woke up around the National Hockey League

—and took notice—it had to be Savard's opponents. His long strides, his thudding bodychecks and his calm in the face of stormy games suggested he could be an all-star in a couple of years.

Apparently Montreal's managing director Sam Pollock felt the same way. Three years ago Pollock had to choose between Savard and Carol Vadnais, another hulking French-Canadian defenseman with abundant talent. The *Habitants* were oozing with talent on the backline and Pollock had to make somebody available in the draft. Although Pollock chose to hold onto Savard, there were times two seasons ago when Serge wasn't quite sure about his future.

"During the first half of the 1968-69 season," Savard said, "I hardly played at all. It was a strange feeling. You go out for one turn but you can't tell if the coach is going to put you out again. So you start worrying. One mistake and you're through for the night."

Serge managed to get on the ice in one way or another in 74 games in 1968-69. He scored eight goals and 23 assists for a total of 31 points. It was a respectable but not especially commanding figure—below the likes of Gilles Marotte and Gary Bergman but above Jim Dorey and Dallas Smith.

When a Montreal writer dared suggest that Savard might someday be in a class with Bobby Orr, D. Leo Monahan of the Boston *Record-American* made it abundantly clear that *THAT* would be the day when Savard could carry Orr's shoes.

Monahan was right until the Canadiens entered the first round of the East Division's 1969 Stanley Cup playoffs against the New York Rangers. All of a sudden Savard became a commanding figure, lugging the puck on long rink-length dashes, playing the stout defensive game and looking like a man who would never need a cold shower to awaken him.

The Canadiens dispatched the Rangers in four straight games and now they were ready for the ultimate test against the Bruins. It would not only decide the East Division champion but also the Stanley Cup winner because everybody knew that the series against the West finalist would be a routine gag.

Montreal won the opening game, 3-2, in sudden death overtime on the home Forum ice but even the staunchest backers of the Flying Frenchmen were willing to concede they were lucky to scrape out on Ralph Backstrom's sudden death goal. The second game also was at The Forum.

Midway in the second period Savard took the ice on a penalty-killing assignment for the Canadiens. The puck was free behind the Montreal net. Savard skated to it, gathered it in on the blade of his stick and began moving out toward the front of the net and goalie Gump Worsley.

It was a time to ice the puck out of danger. Or, at the very least to pass it off to a free teammate. It was *NOT* the time or the place to put on a stickhandling exhibition for the home folks.

But that's exactly what Savard proposed to do.

He accomplished about five feet and two seconds worth of performance when Johnny Bucyk of the Bruins swooped down on him, relieved Serge of the puck and skimmed it across to teammate John McKenzie who took two swings and finally lifted the rubber past Worsley.

It was a classic dum-dum play. What matters is that even Bouchard, Harvey and Reardon have done likewise in their day. And they recovered from the *faux pas*. Savard's mettle would be tested again in the minutes to come. The 24-year-old was not yanked out of the game by his coach, Claude Ruel. Instead Savard came on for the next shift *AND* the one after that.

The Canadiens were trailing by a goal late in the third period. Very late, in fact. Less than two minutes remained when Savard saved the Canadiens the way he saved them with a few key passes in the opening game against Boston.

Montreal organized a massive five-man attack against the Bruin goal but it failed. The Boston offensive unit quickly counterattacked against the temporarily abandoned goalie Gump Worsley. But Savard somehow speeded back and deftly intercepted a pass from Phil Esposito to Ken Hodge.

Once again play turned to the Boston zone. This time the puck went from Yvan Cournoyer to Savard who lifted the disk past goalie Ed Johnston's flying right goal pad and into the corner of the net. Significantly, Bobby Orr was sprawled on his hands and knees at the moment Savard tied the score. Only 69 seconds remained in the period when the red light went on.

"You've got to get a break to do something like that," said Savard. "It was good to get a goal. I figured the first Boston goal was my fault when I tried to carry the puck out instead of shooting it down the ice."

Now the game went into sudden death overtime, and Bruin defenseman Ted Green rapidly took a two-minute penalty for holding when the Canadiens cranked up their power play deep in Bruin territory.

Ralph Backstrom won the decisive face-off from Ed Westfall in the left circle; the puck moved immediately behind Backstrom to John Ferguson, who sent it all the way behind him to the far left blue line where Savard attacked the disk and sent it orbiting toward the Boston net. Mickey Redmond of the Canadiens was standing in front of the goal when Savard shot.

"I had my stick on the ice where it's supposed to be," said Redmond.

Sure enough, Savard's drive caromed off Redmond's blade and zoomed crazily into the air and past the befuddled Johnston.

After two games Savard could boast that (a) he set up all three Montreal goals in the opening match; (b) tied the game in the second contest, and (c) assisted on the sudden death winner in the second game. Suddenly critics began noticing the young man whom coach Ruel had been touting all along.

Serge is an example of the competitive spirit you need in the playoffs," said Ruel. "It is impossible to demand more from him than he gave since the start of the season."

The kudos weren't limited to the Montreal observers either. Harold Kaese, sports columnist of the *Boston Globe*, singled out Savard as the top man in the series.

"Savard," wrote Rex MacLeod, the distinguished writer with the *Toronto Globe and Mail*, "has matured as one of the Canadiens' more accomplished players in the playoffs."

Boston rebounded to win the next two games, 5-0 and 3-2. Savard scored Montreal's second goal in the 3-2 game with 54 seconds remaining and showed no signs of diminishing effort.

The Canadiens then returned home to The Forum, trimmed Boston, 4-2, and set the stage for the sixth and what could be the final game of the series at Boston Garden.

The Bruins took a 1-0 lead on a goal by Ron Murphy early in the game and held on to it with great tenacity through the second period and into the third. But Bruin defenseman Don Awrey took a penalty at 1:05 of the period and the Canadiens' power play went into action again. Captain Jean Beliveau started the play by ladling a pass to Savard at the right point. His long shot sailed toward goalie Gerry Cheevers who happened to be screened by Orr. The puck flew past him and it was a new hockey game. The Canadiens went on to win it on Beliveau's goal in sudden-death overtime.

That set the stage for the Stanley Cup final between St. Louis and Montreal. Nobody expected the Blues to win at The Forum—they blew the first two games by 3-1 scores —but the West Division champs were thought to have a chance in the third game of the series at their own St. Louis Arena. A record crowd of 16,338 on Thursday night, May 1st, turned out for the game.

The score was 0-0 in the first period when Dick Duff of the Canadiens passed the puck to Savard who was astride the St. Louis blue line. "When the Blues' defense opened up," Savard explained, "I kept skating until I was about three strides over their line. One of their defensemen came over to form a partial screen and I let the shot go. I think maybe Jacques Plante saw it too late."

Whether he saw it or not is irrelevant. The puck was in and the Canadiens were off and skating to a 4-0 victory, giving them a 3-0 lead in the series. They wrapped it up on May 4th with a 2-1 win and a four-game sweep of the Cup finale for the second year in a row.

Throughout the Cup finals speculation was rife over which Montreal player would skate off with the Conn Smythe Trophy as the most valuable player. Beliveau, Dick Duff, Rogatien Vachon were all candidates but the favorite remained Savard.

"He did everything for the Canadiens," said Jim

Proudfoot of the *Toronto Daily Star*, "even including a spot of goaltending when the regular netminders got trapped out of position. He played defense, he was point man on the power plays and he moved up to a forward position during most Montreal penalties. He excelled in each role and even found time to contribute some vital scoring plays."

Stafford Smythe, Conn Smythe's son, saw more playoff matches than most of the NHL governors who were to vote on the award. He preferred Duff to Savard.

"Duff played extremely well throughout all three rounds," said Smythe.

"But," Proudfoot countered, "everybody agreed the semi-final against the Bruins was the key series. That's where Savard was best."

Pat Curren of the *Montreal Gazette* dubbed Savard "Superboy" and added that he merited the Smythe Trophy and the $1,500 that goes with it.

As for Serge, he put it this way.

"Ah, the trophy, that would be nice, I suppose, that would be very nice. But there are others. . . ."

Duff did get a vote (Smythe's) but Savard came off with the trophy and the money. The voters were impressed by Savard's four playoff goals, one short of a record by a defenseman. They also dug his six assists in 14 games.

His selection marked the first time one team had two winners and the first time a defenseman won the prize.

The question now is how high the moon for Savard? Can he recover from his injury and stay on Orr's orbit in 1970-71 or was the past year something of a fluke?

Probably something in between. But one thing is certain: Serge Savard won't need Scotty Bowman's cold showers to wake him up anymore.

WALT TKACZUK

His name is unpronounceable.
His style is indefinable.
His ability is questionable.

But somehow Walter Tkaczuk, the New York Rangers' big center, gets the job done; and often better than most third-year men in the National Hockey League.

Tkaczuk (pronounced "Ka-chook") has had his name mis-called ever since he emigrated from Germany in 1949. His parents settled in Northern Ontario and people continued to call him "Walter" rather than try their luck on T-K-A-C-Z-U-K.

Meanwhile the young center was slowly climbing the hockey ladder. First he played in the kids' league around his home in South Porcupine, Ontario.

One day a Ranger scout discovered Walter and transferred him to a more accomplished team. Eventually Tkaczuk made his way to Kitchener of the fast Ontario Hockey Association's Junior A League and it was there that he met Steve Brklacich, who just about ruined Tkaczuk's pronunciation for life.

Brklacich, who happens to be the Rangers' personnel director, was coaching Kitchener at the time. He also had problems with his name (pronounced "Berklazich") so he took the path of least resistance when addressing young Walter. He called him "Taychuk" instead of "Kachook."

"I gave him that 'Taychuk' name," Brklacich admits. "I used to play with a guy named Pete Taychuk and I told Walter it was easier to say than "Ka-chook."

In those days it was virtually impossible to imagine that Tkaczuk, no matter how you pronounced it, would ever confound big-league people with his pronunciation. By hockey standards he was slightly thinner than a darning needle. His skating style was a cross between the lope of the water buffalo and the spring of an elephant. There was nothing in his shot or his defensive play to suggest stardom.

As a matter of fact when he showed up with the Kitchener Rangers one team executive looked him over and with a W. C. Fields' wave of the hand dismissed him with a "G'way boy, ya bother me!"

Fortunately coach Wally Kullman interceded and Tkaczuk was retained. The insight of Kullman is underlined today by the scoring figures. Walt is one of the NHL's top centers and is one-two among the Rangers. But he's more than that.

"If there's a single reason why the Rangers are contenders, it's Tkaczuk," said Boston Bruin goalie Gerry Cheevers. "In one year he became the leader of that club."

Once upon a time—'way back in the early Sixties—the Rangers *HAD* a leader and his name was Andy Bathgate. But when Bathgate was traded to Toronto in February 1964 the Blueshirts became a cooperative society without a real on-ice boss. The Canadiens had Jean Beliveau, the Red Wings had Gordie Howe, but, alas, the poor Rangers.

To be a leader of the Beliveau-Howe genre requires, among other qualities, ability. And if you ask around the NHL dressing rooms you'll be told straight-out that Tkaczuk has it.

"Right now," adds Cheevers, "Tkaczuk is a potential All-Star. He can shoot, he can make plays and he's one of the strongest men I've ever seen on skates. Besides, he's fantastic at winning face-offs."

The center who wins face-offs tilts the game in his team's favor. A hockey team that has the puck is not likely to put it in its own net and when the Tkaczuk-Dave Balon-Bill Fairbairn line is on the ice they usually own the puck with magnetic adhesion.

"Those guys go together like ham'n'eggs," says Francis, "and they keep comin' at you like bulldogs. You watch Tkaczuk; he never takes the Overland Route. He just comin' straight at you."

"I've got some good linemates," says Tkaczuk. "Sometimes it's hard to believe what they can do in the corners."

Others say the same thing about Tkaczuk. Francis likes to compare him with Ted "Teeder" Kennedy, the tenacious Toronto Maple Leaf captain of the late Forties. The signs of Tkaczuk's emerging ability developed in his teens.

"Once when he was only 16 I put him on ice when our club was two men short," says Brklacich. "We were playing Niagara Falls, a powerful team. They had guys like Gilles Marotte, Ron Schock and Bill Goldsworthy. They haven't scored yet."

Walter soon became the hit of Kitchener. The natives liked him because he was—as he is today—a straight-arrow type. Good student; thoughtful, modest and sensitive. "The first thing he did when he got his bonus money," says Kitchener clothier Jack Kronis, "was buy his father a new car."

The Rangers wanted to promote him to the NHL in the 1967-68 season but both management and player hit a temporary impasse and Tkaczuk remained in Kitchener. He came to training camp in 1968 and somehow didn't click the way many observers thought he would. A short stint in Buffalo cured his *malaise* although critics noticed a few flaws in his armor. Flaws that Walter, himself, is quick to acknowledge.

"I don't skate well enough to suit me," he insists. "I don't have a fast enough start. And I don't think my shot is hard enough."

All of which is true. But he has great compensatory values. Lacking rabbit-speed, he takes the shortest route between two points—a straight line—and usually gets to where he's going as fast as his foes. And what his shot lacks in speed it makes up for in accuracy. His scoring record proves that.

"He goes where the puck is," says Brklacich. "He fights for it and when he gets it, he's a hard man to knock off the thing."

Brklacich seems to know everything about his prodigy except how to pronounce his name. This mildly disturbed Mel Woody, the veteran NHL scribe of the Newark Evening News.

"Hard or not," said Woody, "I think you have to make certain concessions to upcoming stars. Like pronouncing their names right."

"I knew Walter would be a good one as soon as he put on a uniform," says Balon. "He's playing as well as any center I've ever played with and that includes some of the best—including Ralph Backstrom and Henri Richard."

Like Backstrom, Tkaczuk learned his hockey in the frigid mining country of Northern Ontario where even snowmen suffer from frostbite. But before Walter landed in Canada he figured prominently in a weird odyssey that started near the end of World War II.

Walter's father, a gold-miner, escaped from the battle-scarred Ukraine and wound up as a displaced person in Emstedetten, Germany. It was there that Walter was born but his father decided it was no place to live. In time he discovered there was mining work to be had in Canada.

He emigrated to Northern Ontario and eventually sent for his wife and child.

Life was rugged in the town of South Porcupine. The winters were long and the summers short. But by comparison with post-war Germany it was a gratifying life for the Tkaczuks. Young Walter went to school, played hockey with the Canadien boys and began developing an unquenchable thirst for the sport.

Had this interest not developed, the chances are he now would be plumbing the depths of The Dome and other mines in the South Porcupine area as he did when he was a teenager accompanying his father.

"I'd go down as far as 3,300 feet," Walt remembers. "Once a man next to my father was crushed in a rock fall. Luckily my father came out of it without a scratch. After a while I gave up mining."Ranger g.m.-coach Emile Francis is grateful for that. He also knows that it's time to pronounce "Ka-chook" correctly.

"I've solved the problem," says Francis. "Now I call him Walter!"

Flashback—Eddie Shore

In March 1970 the National Hockey League presented Eddie Shore with its Lester Patrick Trophy for outstanding service to hockey in the United States.

Shore received the trophy for several reasons, not the least of which being that he built Boston Garden much in the manner that Babe Ruth built Yankee Stadium.

According to many seasoned observers Shore was the best defenseman who ever lived and was much better than the Bruins' current superstar, Bobby Orr.

Shore, himself, obliquely noted that Orr still has not reached Eddie's plane of excellence.

Shore pointed out that while Orr was a "good hockey player" he still required more time in the NHL to really guarantee his ticket to The Hall of Fame. He noted that Orr's bowlegged skating style could cut his career by about four or five years and Shore steadfastly refused to include Orr among the all-time greats.

Such frankness was to be commended but it also suggested why Shore remains one of the most controversial figures hockey has ever known.

Eddie not only was controversial as a player—he nearly killed Ace Bailey of Toronto in an NHL game—but also as the manager and owner of the Springfield Indians of the American Hockey League.

It is doubtful that more fascinating and unbelievable stories could be told about any hockey personality than Shore. Many of them are hilarious, others sombre. But all bear Shore's unusual imprint.

Shore was seven times chosen as a member of the All-Star Team and four times voted its most valuable player. He is a member of the Hall of Fame and has been called "The Babe Ruth of Hockey."

If Ruth built Yankee Stadium, Shore *made* the NHL. He was a rambunctious defenseman who could skate faster than most forwards, hit harder than most Sherman Tanks and pull more people into a rink than any player, living or dead. "He is the only man in hockey generally known to the people who ignore hockey," columnist John Lardner once observed.

Shore played in the NHL from 1926 to 1940. In that time opponents teamed up to cream him, owners sought to outlaw him and fans came to curse him. In 1929 Shore was nearly murdered when a gang of Montreal players bludgeoned him on ice. He lay unconscious for 15 minutes with a broken nose, three cracked teeth, a gash on his cheekbone, a two-inch cut over his left eye and two black eyes.

In 1933 Shore nearly killed Toronto forward Ace Bailey by hitting him from behind—just how illegal and how deliberate the check was remains debatable to this day—and ended Bailey's hockey career.

The Toronto player suffered a cerebral concussion and for eight days his life teetered on the brink of death. He eventually recovered and Shore was exonerated. Eddie went on to score 263 points in his first ten seasons, also a league record.

From time to time Shore feuded with Bruin manager Art Ross. By 1940 Shore had had it with Ross. He took his money and bought the Springfield franchise. Ross immediately sold him to the New York Americans. The result was undoubtedly the world's record for commuting. Shore played for Springfield on Saturday night, with the Americans on Sunday and took a breather on Monday.

Shore had paid $42,000 for the Indians—$16,000 in cash and the rest on a note—and he wasn't about to squander a penny if he could help it. "When he first got the franchise," says Jack Riley, President of the Pittsburgh Penguins, "he used to park the cars outside the arena 'til about ten minutes before game time, then he'd go in and play the game."

"He used to have the players take inner tubes from their automobile tires, cut them up into rubber bands and put them around the hockey stockings to save buying tape. During the ice show Eddie operated one of the spotlights himself to save expenses."

On the other hand he thought nothing of donating the Springfield Coliseum ice free of charge to Springfield youngsters who developed into some of the best players in the United States.

When considering Shore's demands on his players, one must recall that Shore was terribly demanding on Shore, the player. His body was skewered in so many places more than 900 stitches were required to hold it together. His back, hip and collarbone were fractured, both eyeballs were split open, every tooth knocked out of his mouth and his nose was broken 14 times. His jaw was cracked five times and his ear was once sliced by a sharp skate like a piece of liver under a butcher's knife. Shore went from doctor to doctor until he found one who would sew it up rather than amputate. The doctor finally performed the embroidery under Eddie's instruction.

Shore's thirst for hockey was unquenchable. Once enroute to the railroad station to join his teammates on the ride from Boston to Montreal he was entangled in a traffic jam. By the time Eddie reached the station the train had gone. Those were the days when it was impossible to obtain air transportation. It appeared that Shore would miss the game. Instead he requisitioned a wealthy friend's limousine, replete with chauffeur, and at midnight commanded the driver to head for Montreal.

Unfortunately a blizzard hit Boston and the driver had trouble even getting the car out of the suburbs. Shore finally insisted that he be permitted to handle the car and the chauffeur obliged.

Shore directed the car on an odyssey that defies the imagination. Remember, this was in the late Twenties and there were no super highways. Soon the windshield wipers stopped wiping so Shore simply removed the windshield altogether. The pair survived a couple skids into ditches—once a French-Canadian farmer hauled them out with the help of his mare—and ploughed their way North. When they finally arrived in Montreal it was 5 p.m. the following afternoon and Shore's hand was so frozen to the wheel he couldn't unbend it. Art Ross sent him to bed with orders not to come to the rink.

Needless to say, Shore *DID* show up, played nearly the entire game and get this, scored the winning goal!

Many of the present NHL players are loaded with their favorite Shore stories because many of them learned their trade—for better, or worse—in Springfield.

Ken Schinkel of the Pittsburgh Penguins tells one about the time Shore berated him during a practice session. Normally mild-mannered, Schinkel was upset because his wife had just lost a baby. "Eddie," Schinkel shouted in front of the entire squad, "you can go to hell."

"That'll cost you $100," snapped Shore.

After the playoffs Schinkel dropped into the hockey office to say goodbye to his boss. "Wait a minute," said Shore, digging into his pocket and pulling out $100 in bills. "I don't know why I'm so good to you."

Shore always fancied himself an amateur doctor and claimed he twice cured himself of cancer; once of the bowels and once of the liver. "All I can say," Shore once remarked, "is that three specialists once gave me three months to live—and that was in 1940."

One afternoon Shore noticed that Schinkel was sniffling. The player had a common cold and, having tried the usual remedies without success, resigned himself to waiting out the ailment. But Shore had other ideas. "You know what he prescribed," said Schinkel, "twelve drops of iodine. And you know what, it worked!"

Another NHLer with vivid memories of Shore is Billy McCreary of the St. Louis Blues. McCreary had a four year dose of Shore, which, apparently was four years too many. He finally threatened to quit hockey altogether and Shore finally traded McCreary to Hull-Ottawa. As soon as Billy arrived in Ottawa he reacted as if he had been sprung from prison. One of the first to talk with him was Jack Kinsella, then sports columnist of the Ottawa *Citizen*.

"Springfield," said McCreary, "is the absolute end of the line. I was so fed up with the way Shore treated his players I decided to get outa the game and take a regular job."

McCreary claimed that Shore was so cheap, he'd make Jack Benny look like the last of the great spenders. "We were on strict budgets with him," said McCreary. "He allowed us to tip taxi drivers 15 cents. After a while we got so well known around the league none of the cabbies wanted to pick us up.

"That was bad enough. But some guys had a bonus clause in their contracts. If they got, say, 30 goals, they'd get more money. So a guy would be comin' close to 30 near the end of the season. Does he make it? Hell, Shore would sit him out of the last five games so he couldn't score anymore. And if you think I'm joking, just ask any player who skated for Shore."

I once read Kinsella's column about McCreary to Shore and asked him for his version. "There are not too many like him," said Shore. "I would say most our players are happy. McCreary resented many things. He wanted a major league salary but he couldn't play as well as the other two men on his line. I think you'll find a few like McCreary in every walk of life. They're not satisfied because they're not as good as they want to be."

Opposing coaches often suffered more anguish than some of Shore's employees. When Toronto Maple Leafs' vice president King Clancy was coaching Cincinnati, Shore said he'd allow Clancy use of the Springfield ice in the morning. The Coliseum is a barn-like structure with rows of windows near the ceiling on either side of the ice. Late in the morning the sun beams through the windows giving the rink its only feeling of warmth. But this, of course, is contingent on a sunny day.

At the time, Emile Francis, the New York Rangers g.m.-coach, was playing goal for Cincinnati and remembered skating out on the rink at 9 a.m.

"The place was dark as the Dickens," Francis recalls, "so I asked Clancy to get the lights put on. Just then, Shore comes by.

" 'Hey, Eddie,' Clancy yells, 'how about giving us some light for the practice?' "

"Ya know what Shore tells 'em. He says, "Wait a half-hour 'til the sun rises and comes through the windows. Then you'll have plenty of light'."

Clancy obtained his revenge the following night. A few seconds after the referee dropped the puck to start the game, he climbed over the boards, marched solemnly across the rink and presented Shore with a lantern!

Shore was especially rough on his goaltenders. "I'll

never forget how Eddie hated to see his goalkeepers fall to the ice," said Don Simmons, who played for Springfield, Boston, Toronto and New York. "If he got a player and that poor sap fell down to block a shot Shore would get a piece of twine and tie the goalie's arm to the crossbar of the net. Then he'd dare him to fall."

Simmons was traumatized one night in a game against Cleveland. Referee Frank Udvari called a penalty against Springfield that so enraged Shore he ordered his entire team off the ice—with the exception of Simmons.

The referee pulled out his watch. "You've got ten seconds to ice a team," Udvari warned Shore. "Then I drop the puck, no matter what."

Shore ignored the threat. "Ten-nine-eight. . . ." The seconds ticked away but Shore was unrelenting. The crowd gasped as Udvari dropped the puck and five Cleveland players tore up the ice at the beleaguered Simmons. So astonished were the attackers at this unheard of opportunity, they fought among themselves over who would take the shot. Finally, Bo Elik of Cleveland got off a drive that missed. Three succeeding shots were so hurried that they went wide until Simmons pounced on a rebound and stopped play. Udvari pulled out his watch again but this time Shore dispatched his men to the ice.

"Every hockey player should have had a chance to play for Shore," said Springfield alumnus Don Johns, "just to know what hell is like. If they survived they always had something to tell their grandchildren."

As a teacher of hockey Shore was without peer. "He'd bug his players over three points," said Baltimore Clipper scout Aldo Guidolin. "He'd want the hands two feet apart on the stick; the feet 11 inches apart on the ice and he'd want you to skate in a sort of sitting position. If you didn't do that you'd be in big trouble."

Once during a practice Guidolin was congratulating himself for what he considered a perfect pass that resulted in a goal. Shore blew his whistle and beckoned Guidolin while teammates gaped. "Mis-ter Guidolin," he asked, "do you know what you did wrong?"

"The pass was perfect," Aldo replied, "I was in a sitting position. My two hands were on the stick. What more do you want?"

"Mi-ster Guidolin," Shore asserted in his slow, deliberate manner, that would frighten a lion, "your legs were *two inches* too far apart!"

Shore might still be in Springfield today instead of retirement had he not pressed his players too far. The showdown came about in the 1966-67 season when hockey players turned to attorney R. Alan Eagleson for advice on unionization.

Springfield's players had an assortment of gripes with Shore and when the Indians' owner adamantly rebuffed them they turned to Eagleson. "I don't quite know what we can do in Springfield," Eagleson said at the time, "but it's clear that reform is urgent there."

Eagleson counseled against a complete walkout and attempted to negotiate with Shore, which is like carrying on a lively dialogue with The Sphinx at Ghiza. Meanwhile the Indians were in a general state of depression.

"The team appears to be in such decay, in fact, that gangrene has set in," wrote Dick Beddoes in the *Toronto Globe and Mail*. "The players are so disenchanted with Shore they seem to malinger."

To which Eagleson added, "Apparently we've got to correct the working conditions in Springfield, and wherever else hockey players are quasi-peons."

Eventually the feud came to a head and Shore lost one of the few battles of his life, although he did collect a pretty penny when the Springfield franchise was dealt to the Los Angeles Kings of the NHL's West Division.

Nevertheless he left a legacy of laughs and thrills, fuss and fanfare, enmity and admiration.

Obviously the Lester Patrick Trophy award committee prefers to look at the more positive side of Shore. Who can blame them? It's too bad, though, that old Lester isn't around today to make the presentation.

He and Eddie would have put their arms around each other and laughed uproariously over the favorite Patrick-Shore story of all.

It happened in the late Twenties when Eddie was Mister Hockey and the envy of every team in the league, especially New York's Rangers. At the time Col. John S. Hammond was president of the Rangers and had his eyes on Shore. One day he called his manager, Patrick, into his office and very naively asked Lester if Shore could help the Rangers.

"Of course he would, Colonel," Patrick responded.

Col. Hammond then insisted that he would wire Bruin president Charles Adams and offer him $5,000 and second-string defenseman Myles J. Lane (now a justice of the New York State Supreme Court) for Shore. It was as preposterous an offer as Patrick could have imagined but he had to follow through and the telegram was dispatched to Adams.

A day later, Adams wired the following reply:

"YOU ARE SO MANY MYLES FROM SHORE YOU NEED A LIFE PRESERVER!"

Hockey's Fast-Growing I.Q.

Manager Tommy Ivan of the Chicago Black Hawks stunned his National Hockey League colleagues at the start of the 1969-70 season when he announced that his team would open the season with no less than three recent college-graduates on the Windy City varsity.

They were defenseman Keith Magnuson and forwards Jim Wiste and Cliff Koroll, each of whom was a graduate of Denver University.

Ivan's decision was regarded as suicidal to say the least. Everybody who was anybody in the NHL realized that college-trained hockey players required, at the very least, two or three years to acclimatize themselves to the pros. Magnuson and his fraternity brothers immediately went about the business of destroying this ice shibboleth. And they did it in spades.

Magnuson, especially, underlined the fact that hockey moguls had long been making a big mistake in overlooking collegiate stars. Red-headed Keith proved that a player with a good head could accomplish as much—if not more —than a player who relied on speed and brawn.

But Magnuson wasn't alone. His teammate Koroll, played a solid season for Chicago and goaltender Tony Esposito, himself a graduate of Michigan Tech, went on to set a new record for shutouts and became the league's best rookie.

All of this served to magnify the point that major league hockey's overall I. Q. is on the rise, and it is a good thing. For too many years the NHL was held up to ridicule as an organization that placed a heavy emphasis on dumbness. The stupider you were, the better the hockey player you'd be; or so the theory went.

In December 1968 a respected Canadian magazine published a full-page caricature of the typical big-league hockey player. Its legs and arms were elephantine but the head was minuscule.

"The brain," said the attached caption, "is composed of one small hockey puck. The favorite expression is 'DUHHHHH—which way did he go? Which way did he go? Which way did he go?"

At the very least the caricature suggested that NHL players, generally speaking, are in great need of an esthetic lobotomy. The title of the article labelled them "Big, Fast and Dumb" and, surprise of surprises, was co-authored by none other than R. Alan Eagleson, executive director of the NHL Players Association and Bobby Orr's chief advisor.

This super put-down of the collective intellect of hockey players exaggerated to make a point and the point is quite clear—hockey players are the least educated and least sophisticated of pro athletes.

Consider the facts. Less than 25 per cent of the NHL players are high school graduates and that includes superstars such as Bobby Orr, Gordie Howe, and Bobby Hull.

By comparison 75 per cent of pro football players are college graduates while in basketball the per centage is more than 60 per cent.

It is a situation that has galled Eagleson and other progressive hockey people who believe the NHL owners have exploited their players at the expense of their education. Henri Richard of the Montreal Canadiens explained:

"Most of us don't have much education because we had to quit school to play hockey. When we went into the office to sign our contracts the club had lawyers and accountants—we had ourselves."

Richard's case is typical. Nearly all NHL players have graduated through junior A hockey leagues. The pressure of junior A competition is so intense it is difficult even for the gifted athlete to concentrate on his studies.

"But hockey," said Eagleson, "takes its anti-education attitude a disgusting step further by raiding young Canadian boys in the middle of their high-school years. Pro teams are constantly persuading promising teenaged prospects to move from their home towns to cities where the teams maintain junior A farm clubs."

Once moved to the new surroundings the player tends to concentrate on his hockey and eschew his studies. It's an almost inevitable fact of life. It happened to Orr when he moved from Parry Sound to Oshawa, Ontario, and it happened to Hull when he was transferred from Pointe Anne to St. Catherine, Ontario.

Eagleson and others argue that NHL clubs have a minimal interest in encouraging their players' education.

"In fact," he noted, "most teams are downright impatient to whisk their boys out of the classroom and onto the rinks. To them a university education is excess baggage."

The NHL Establishment, of course, refutes these charges. The front office has a pile of statistics describing how teams spent thousands of dollars sending lads through school while they were furthering their junior hockey.

This, however, is not a matter of choice. The teams did this because there was no other way to guarantee they'd retain the young man as a hockey player. If they didn't assure his parents he'd be educated the chances were the parents would switch him to another team that did offer it.

There are indications that the age of the Neanderthal hockey player is disappearing. Thanks to Eagleson, whose influence among stickhandlers is more pronounced than that of the owners, a university education is becoming an essential item in their thinking.

As a result the number of college men in the NHL is increasing. Bob Pulford, Carl Brewer, Red Berenson and Lou Angotti are among the veterans who have their Bachelor degrees.

For Pulford and Brewer it didn't come easy. Both handled their studies while playing in the NHL. Both Berenson and Angotti attended college first—much to the displeasure of the NHL clubs—and then made the jump to the NHL.

Early last year Wren Blair, general manager of the Minnesota North Stars, pointed out that Berenson's four years at the University of Michigan stunted his hockey growth even though Red was an All-America center.

Berenson represents the new breed which puts education ahead of hockey. Danny O'Shea, one of Blair's North Stars, fought the NHL's attempts to turn him pro years ago. Instead he signed up with Canada's National Team in Winnipeg and went to the University of Manitoba.

O'Shea's decision was symbolic of the relentless trend toward studies among hockey players. Brian Conacher is another. He helped the Toronto Maple Leafs to a Stanley Cup victory in 1966-67 and appeared to be one of the most promising forwards in the NHL. Instead of continuing his big-league career he quit hockey in 1968-69 and pursued courses at the University of Western Ontario.

By then it became apparent to NHL moguls they were fighting a losing battle with the educational process. Expansion compelled them to mine new areas for talent, so they turned to the universities for help.

"Player training and development will become more closely oriented with educational facilities through scholarships," predicts NHL President Clarence Campbell. "Demand for accommodation at U.S. colleges by native players plus the handicap imposed by U. S. college rules will curtail current Canadian migration to the U. S. on scholarships and will intensify demand for admission to Canadian universities."

Translated, it means the NHL already has read the handwriting on the wall. In the old days the big league wouldn't waste its time with a college man if it could help it. Now it realizes that college players can be as good, if not better, than their less-educated counterparts.

Wherever you look these days, you'll find college grads dotting the lineups of NHL teams. Which raises the question: does higher education help or hurt a big league player?

Another brainy hockey player is defenseman Arnie Brown of the Rangers. Brown completed more than a year of courses at the University of Ottawa and is capable of discussing such esoteric subjects as Johnny Cash's lyrics, fishing off St. Croix and the Black Revolution without discomfort.

"On the whole the hockey player image is changing," said Brown. "Mainly it's because everyone is becoming more worldly, more aware. Years ago, for example, a fellow would come to New York, play his hockey and go home. Now we're taking advantage of the city. But you can't say a hockey player should have a certain plane of intelligence. One should never put oneself above anybody else on those grounds."

Of course the mere possession of a college degree assures a man nothing in the way of common sense, let alone brains. Gordie Howe and Bobby Hull, though lacking diplomas, are articulate, witty men, capable of holding forth with Ph.D.'s. Both admit they should have finished their schooling and Howe compensated for his educational shortcomings by becoming an avid reader and crossword puzzle expert.

Bobby Orr told me his mother urged him to finish grade 12 (Canada's equivalent of a high school diploma) but the pressures of hockey intervened. The Bruin superstar vowed he would finish his last year of high school in Boston during the 1968-69 season but there was no time for it.

Since Bobby will be a millionaire before he's thirty the need for a solid education is less relevant than for the fringe players who never know when they'll be bounced out of pro hockey.

Eagleson was supremely prophetic when he said, "I'm convinced that this new awareness that education comes first is eventually going to turn the entire structure of professional hockey on its ear."

It has and not all for the good.

All-America goalie Ken Dryden rejected a Montreal Canadiens' contract to go to law school and play for the Canadian National Team in 1969.

Bill "Red" Hay walked out on the NHL at the prime of his hockey life to take an engineering job.

On the other hand there are collegians like Wiste, Koroll and Magnuson who jumped to the NHL and gave the sport the sophistication it merits.

The Lighter Side of Hockey

Hockey encyclopedists may not be aware of this but the first good hockey story has been traced back to the prehistoric game between the Boston Neanderthals and the Pittsburgh Paleozoics. George Oop, cousin of Alley, accidentally knocked a dinosaur skull—then the official puck —into his own net and the first big guffaw was heard round the league.

Since then there's been many a laugh around the ice box and one of the best involves Hec Fowler, a darn good goalie who played for the Victoria Cougars and Boston Bruins among numerous clubs. As netminders go, Fowler never betrayed a weakness on the ice; it was his off-ice hang-up that was his greatest problem. Old Hec, it turns out, was an inveterate fire buff. One night while his club was preparing to go out on the ice Fowler, sure enough, was missing. He had taken off to help fight a blaze around the corner.

Speaking of missing persons, how about the night in the mid-Forties when Toronto's Ted Kennedy and Bob Davidson were sprinting down the ice against the Canadiens at The Forum. Kennedy, the center, skimmed the puck to Davidson on left wing and then broke for the Montreal net. When Kennedy next looked up he was astonished to discover that Davidson was gone. A pair of fanatic Forum rooters had hauled him over the boards and were grappling with the Leaf behind the rail seats.

The subject of more funny stories than any hockey player of his time was Jean Baptiste Pusie, a huge French-Canadian who played briefly in the NHL but spent much of his time breaking them up in the minors.

Pusie had a thin temper and one night he took exception to a railside critic who had some choice words to say about Jean's French-Canadian lineage. Pusie vaulted the boards and pursued his now fleeing antagonist. Down the aisle they went but Jean was hampered by his cumbersome skates and equipment.

Undaunted, Pusie dashed after the man through the rink's lobby and then out onto the street. The effect of steel blade on sidewalk was even more of an impediment than it was on the rubber matting of the rink and after two blocks of running Pusie finally gave up the chase.

Unfortunately Jean's teammates never regained his services that night. Rather than return to the arena he stepped into a convenient watering spot and consoled himself over a beer for the rest of the night.

Bruin fans with good memories still chuckle over a fast one Boston manager Art Ross pulled on his Ranger counterpart, Lester Patrick, in the Thirties. Seems that Ross figured the old Madison Square Garden Rink was too cramped for his free-wheeling Bruins. What to do?

"Tell you what," Ross told his men in the dressing room before the game. "I want somebody to go out there and punch Bill. Cook right on the nose. That way we'll at least get a Ranger and a Bruin off the ice and we'll have more room."

The first to try it was Red Beattie but he never could get to Cook before his turn was completed. Then there was a line change and this time Alex Smith went over the boards and took dead aim at the high-scoring right wing. Bop! Smith rapped Cook on the proboscis. Enraged, Bill's brother, Bun, dashed over to Smith and jumped him. By the time order was restored, Smith and the two Cooks each had themselves a penalty.

And, of course, Ross had the last laugh. Thanks to his ploy the Bruins won by a goal.

Of the contemporary players, Bob Plager of the St. Louis Blues ranks among the better practical jokers of hockey. During the 1967-1968 season Plager executed a remarkable embarrassment on teammate Ray Fortin, a French-Canadien defenseman with a poor grasp of English.

Plager's initial move was to pilfer Fortin's false teeth. The Blues were in Philadelphia at the time, so Plager mailed Fortin's falsies from Philly to St. Louis. "It was kind of funny to see him walking around town for two days without eating," said Plager. "Ah, he was a trouble-maker anyway, who began hiding socks almost as soon as he got here. He probably deserved it."

Deserve it not, Fortin soon developed a sore throat and then laryngitis. He could hardly make himself heard and felt obliged to learn the English word for sore-throat so that he could at least try to explain his plight.

So, Fortin asked Plager how to say sore throat and Plager told him; except, instead of telling him sore throat, Plager substituted an obscenity that would stun a long-shoreman's ear. It took Fortin about five minutes to real-ize what had been inflicted on him. Whenever Ray tried telling someone he had a sore-throat the other would turn away in horror.

"Well," laughed Plager, "he learned *some* English any-way!"

If that sounds implausible, how about this yarn—sworn to be the truth—about ex-Ranger "Wild Bill" Ezinicki, the one-time NHL badman who is now an accomplished professional golfer. Affable Ezzie gets as much kick out of telling it as I did hearing it when Bill played in the Garden during the 1954-1955 season.

"It happened in the forties," said Ezzie, "when I was still playing junior hockey in Oshawa, Ontario. Those were the war years and liquor was hard to come by. Well, anyway, a club official decided to take me to Toronto to watch a Stanley Cup game and he phoned ahead to a sporting goods dealer to get a pair of tickets.

"In those days you were allowed one twelve-ounce bottle of liquor a month according to the war ration laws. They called it a 'Mickey'.

"When my friend phoned the sporting goods fellow he said 'I'm bringing Ezinicki with me.' But the guy in To-ronto thought he said he was bringing a 'Mickey' not Ezinicki.

"The sporting goods guy told a few friends to hang around the store because some good liquor was on the way. When we finally arrived, the guy said, 'Okay, haul out the Mickey!'

"My friend was amazed, 'Who said anything about a Mickey,' he said. 'I told you I was bringing Ezinicki'."

According to Wild Bill, the semantic snafu nearly ended a lovely friendship.

Needless to say, our abused friends, the referees, retain an excellent humor quotient, which is why they perform so capably. One of the funniest arbiters was Georges Gravel, a wonderful French-Canadian who was as bald as a man *could* be bald. In fact, Gravel was as funny as he was hairless. Which was very.

A typical Gravel quip sputtered out in the middle of a Red Wing-Canadien game. Having failed to split the Montreal defense, a Detroit player pitched forward in a swan dive and lay face down on the ice hoping Gravel would give the Canadiens a penalty. But Georges was no fool.

He skated to the fallen athlete and laconically observed:

"Why don't you get up? Don't you know you're melting the ice beneath you?"

Know Your Hockey

Ed Linn, the respected author of numerous sports books, once unnerved the hockey world by writing an article lampooning hockey's rules. The story was called "What's the Blue Line For?" It didn't exactly answer the question, but perhaps we can here—and tell you about some of hockey's other rules.

THE RINK

All rinks are not standardized. And even if they were, they would not be identical because some boards which surround a rink are lively, others dull; some stiff, some resilient. And some ice surfaces are slicker than others.

As nearly as possible, a rink should be 200 feet long, 85 feet wide. For example, the Forum rink in Vancouver (as all new NHL arenas) is 200 feet by 85 feet. Where it is shorter than some is in the center or neutral zone, since the blue lines which divide the rink into three zones should be drawn 60 feet from the goal lines.

The red line which splits the neutral zone is 12 inches wide. It came into being in 1943-44. The purpose: to speed up the game, make it possible to pass forward half the length of the rink without being offside, that is, from one's own defense zone to the red line.

The texture of ice itself varies from rink to rink. The Forum's surface is about five-eighths of an inch thick and is considered fast. In those areas where ice is kept on longer, it is usually thicker and slower.

Each rink has similar ice markings, spots and circles. Most face-offs take place on the spots. The circles are at center ice, and one to either side of each goal. Four other spots are in the neutral zone. The circles are 30 feet in diameter, and only the two players facing off are permitted within the circles.

EQUIPMENT

Hockey sticks, like baseball bats, are lighter than they used to be. Also more flexible, with more whip action. They're made of northern white ash or rock elm. Sticks may not exceed 53 inches from heel to the end of the shaft.

A goalie's pads can't be as wide as he might like them to be, not more than 10 inches wide, and the blade of a goalie's stick shall not exceed three and a half inches, except at the heel, where it can be an extra inch wide.

All protective equipment except gloves, headgear and goalkeeper's leg guards must be worn under the uniform. Much of this is cushioned with foam rubber.

ON BEING OFFSIDE

A team on the offense is twice restricted in their forward passes up ice.

A player in his own zone can pass up to the red line. If he's in the neutral zone, he can pass over the red line but not over the opponent's blue line.

Fans often think they see an offside when a pass is made from the defensive zone to a teammate on the red line or the opponent's blue line. The determining factor is the skates of the player on the receiving end, not his stick or the puck. If just one of the player's skates is not over the line, he is on side. However, if it gets too confusing just remember that the basic idea of the game is to put the puck in the net, and the best idea for a fan is to keep your eyes on the puck.

The puck must always precede the player over the red line and then the attacking blue line.

Often you will see a player jam on the brakes and straddle a line until his teammate carries or shoots the puck over the line.

"ICING" THE PUCK

The puck itself shall be made of vulcanized rubber, or other approved material, one inch thick and three inches in diameter, and shall weigh between five and a half ounces and six ounces.

"Icing," itself occurs when a team shoots the puck from its own side of the red line over the opponent's goal line (not into the goal, of course).

The puck is then brought back for a face-off deep in the zone of the offending team.

There are four conditions when icing is not called:

(a) When a team is shorthanded as a result of a penalty, it cannot be called icing.

(b) When a defending opponent, in the judgment of the officials, could have played the puck before it crossed his own goal line, there shall be no icing.

(c) If the puck cuts across part of the rectangle in front of the goal, a rectangle called the crease, no icing shall be called.

(d) When a member of the team which ices the puck touches it before the defending opponent, no icing is called and play continues.

SCORING

Scoring a goal is the so-called name of the game. It is not necessary to shoot the puck into the netting behind the goalie to score. If the entire puck crosses the goal line inside the posts, it's a goal:

(a) *Unless* an attacking player kicks the puck, or throws the puck, or otherwise deliberately directs the puck into the goal by any means other than the stick.

(b) *Unless* an attacking player is in the goal crease, and is in no way held in by a defender, while a teammate "scores."

It is within the rules for an attacking player to carry the puck into the goal-crease area and still score.

It is also within the rules for an attacking side to score a goal by having a shot deflect off a teammate, as long as the teammate does not intentionally steer the deflection into the goal.

If that same shot deflects into the goal off a defender, or if a defender inadvertently directs the puck over the goal line, it's a goal.

While a goal does not count if it is kicked in by an attacker, if that same attacker kicks it in off a defender other than the goalie, it does count. In this case, the kicker is credited with the goal. On the other hand, if a shot is deflected in off a teammate, the teammate gets credit for the goal and the shooter gets an assist.

No more than two assists shall be credited on any goal, and those assists go to the two players who handle the puck immediately preceding the goal.

GAME OFFICIALS

Once upon a time, a hockey game was run by two referees working together. They were their own linesmen. Now there is one referee and two linesmen.

The referee controls the game. He calls all the penalties and must decide the legality of the goals, though sometimes he will call time and ask his linesmen for an opinion before he makes a final decision.

The duty of the linesmen is to determine offsides and icings. They drop the puck for face-offs. They chase the pucks after stoppage of play. And it is their unenviable job to break up fights while the referee assesses the penalties.

THE GOAL NETS

A goal net, or cage, is six feet wide and four feet high. The NHL's officially approved and adopted net is named after Art Ross, its inventor, and former manager of the Boston Bruins.

It is designed so that pucks entering the net will stay in, though occasionally a shot will rebound off a back post and carom out. The goal line itself is two inches wide.

In front of each goal: the goal crease. It's drawn by a red line a foot to the side of each goal post and four feet out, a rectangle designed to minimize traffic in front of the goalie.

And behind each goal sits a goal judge whose only responsibility is to decide whether the puck crosses the goal line in front of him. If it does, he pushes a button which lights up the red lamp overhead.

THE PENALTIES

There are five classifications: (a) minor penalties. (b) bench minor penalties. (c) misconduct penalties. (d) match penalties. (e) penalty shot.

A *minor penalty* calls for two minutes and can be imposed on any player including the goalie. However, if a goalie is called, a substitute may sit out his penalty.

A *bench minor penalty* involves removal from the ice of a player of the team called for the penalty for a period of two minutes.

If while a team is shorthanded by one or more minor or bench minor penalties the opposing team scores, the first of such penalties shall automatically terminate. There is no exception. If a shorthanded team incurs a penalty shot against it, and the penalty shot succeeds, a player is sprung from the penalty box.

A *misconduct penalty* is a 10-minute penalty, generally called against a player who becomes abusive in language or gesture. It puts him out for 10 minutes, but does not leave his team shorthanded. It is also accompanied by an automatic $25 fine against the offender.

A *match penalty* means ejection from the game. It's levied for (a) deliberate attempt to injure, wherein a sub can be used after five minutes, or (b) deliberate injury to an opponent, calling for 10 minutes without replacement plus an automatic $100 fine.

The *penalty shot*, seldom invoked, gives a player a clear shot at goal with only the goalie to defend. It's called chiefly when a player is fouled from behind (not from a side swipe), when he has a clear path to the goal.

At no time is a team asked to play shorthanded by more than two men, even if its penalty box is jammed to overflowing. There are, of course, separate penalty boxes for each side.

THE FOULS

They come in many ways, these fouls, and some are regarded by players as much more offensive than others. Spearing, for instance, can be a minor (two minutes) or a major (five) or even a match penalty, and means what it says: using the point of the stick blade to stab an opponent.

Other penalties, usually minors, are called checking into the boards, charging, cross-checking, elbowing, high-sticking, holding, hooking, interference, kneeing, slashing and, most common of all, tripping.

Most of these are self-explanatory, but depend on official interpretation, and sometimes on the degree of violence. For instance, a player can be "ridden off" along the boards but cannot be slammed into the boards.

A minor penalty is sometimes changed to a major penalty if blood is drawn, but this again is a matter of judgment. Conversely, some fights are adjudged to be roughing, an offender drawing two minutes, or four instead of five.

Referees have different signals for different penalties. For instance, he'll grab his left wrist with right hand to denote holding.

BERENSON, GORDON ARTHUR (RED)
Born, Regina, Sask., December 8, 1939.
Center. Shoots left. 6', 190 lbs.
Last amateur club: University of Michigan.

Season	Club	Lea	Regular Schedule					Playoffs				
			GP	G	A	TP	PIM	GP	G	A	TP	PIM
1961-62	Mtl. Canadiens	NHL	4	1	2	3	4	5	2	0	2	0
1962-63	Hull-Ottawa	EPHL	30	23	25	48	28	—	—	—	—	—
1962-63	Mtl. Canadiens	NHL	37	2	6	8	15	5	0	0	0	0
1963-64	Mtl. Canadiens	NHL	69	7	9	16	12	7	0	0	0	4
1964-65	Quebec	AHL	65	22	34	56	16	5	1	2	3	8
1964-65	Mtl. Canadiens	NHL	3	1	2	3	0	9	0	1	1	2
1965-66	Quebec	AHL	34	17	36	53	14	6	1	5	6	2
1965-66	Mtl. Canadiens	NHL	23	3	4	7	12					
1966-67	NY Rangers	NHL	30	0	5	5	2	4	0	1	1	2
1967-68	NY Rangers	NHL	19	2	1	3	2					
	St. Louis	NHL	55	22	29	51	22	18	5	2	7	9
1968-69	St. Louis	NHL	76	35	47	82	43	12	7	3	10	20
1969-70	St. Louis	NHL	67	33	39	72	38	16	7	5	12	8
	NHL Totals		383	106	144	250	150	76	21	12	33	45

CHEEVERS, GERALD MICHAEL (GERRY)
Born, St. Catharines, Ont., December 7, 1940.
Goaltender. Shoots left. 5'11", 185 lbs.
Last amateur club: St. Michaels College (Jrs.).

Season	Club	Lea	Regular Schedule				Playoffs			
			GP	GA	SO	GAPG	GP	GA	SO	GAPG
1961-62	Toronto	NHL	2	7	0	3.60	—	—	—	—
1961-62a	Sault Ste. Marie	EPHL	29	103	1	3.55	—	—	—	—
1961-62	Pitt.-Rochester	AHL	24	84	1	3.50	2	8	0	4.00
1962-63	Rochester	AHL	19	75	1	3.95	—	—	—	—
1962-63a	Sudbury	EPHL	51	212	0	4.15	8	29	*1	3.62
1963-64a	Rochester	AHL	66	187	3	2.84	2	8	0	4.00
1964-65ab	Rochester	AHL	72	195	*5	2.68	10	24	0	2.34
1965-66	Boston	NHL	5⅔	34	0	6.00				
1965-66	Oklahoma City	CPHL	29⅓	73	3	2.49	9	19	0	*2.11
1966-67	Boston	NHL	17⅓	62	1	3.64				
1966-67c	Oklahoma City	CPHL	25⅓	71	1	2.80	11	29	*1	*2.64
1967-68d	Boston	NHL	44	125	3	2.83	4	15	0	3.75
1968-69	Boston	NHL	52	145	3	2.80	9⅔	16	*3	1.68
1969-70	Boston	NHL	41	108	4	2.72	13	29	0	2.23
	NHL Totals		162	481	11	2.97	26⅔	60	3	2.25

a Received one assist.
b Won Harry Holmes Memorial Trophy.
c Won CPHL Leading Goalkeeper Award.
d Received two assists.

Drafted by Boston from Toronto, June 9, 1965.

ESPOSITO, PHIL ANTHONY

Born, Sault Ste. Marie, Ont., February 20, 1942.
Center. Shoots left. 6'1", 195 lbs.
Last amateur club: St. Catharines (Jrs.).

Season	Club	Lea	Regular Schedule					Playoffs				
			GP	G	A	TP	PIM	GP	G	A	TP	PIM
1961-62	Sault Ste. Marie	EPHL	6	0	3	3	2	--	--	--	--	--
1962-63	St. Louis	EPHL	71	36	54	90	51	--	--	--	--	--
1963-64	St. Louis	CPHL	43	26	54	80	65	--	--	--	--	--
1963-64	Chicago	NHL	27	3	2	5	2	4	0	0	0	0
1964-65	Chicago	NHL	70	23	32	55	44	13	3	3	6	15
1965-66	Chicago	NHL	69	27	26	53	49	6	1	1	2	2
1966-67	Chicago	NHL	69	21	40	61	40	6	0	0	0	7
1967-68	Boston	NHL	74	35	*49	84	21	4	0	3	3	0
1968-69abcd	Boston	NHL	74	49	*77	*126	79	10	*8	*10	*18	8
1969-70	Boston	NHL	76	43	56	99	50	57	25	31	56	48
	NHL Totals		459	201	282	483	285	14	13	14	27	16

a Won Art Ross Trophy.
b Won Hart Trophy.
c NHL record for assists in regular season.
d NHL record for points in regular season.

Traded to **Boston** by **Chicago** with Ken Hodge and Fred Stanfield for Gilles Marotte, Pit Martin and Jack Norris, May 15, 1967.

ESPOSITO, ANTHONY JAMES (TONY)

Born, Sault Ste. Marie, Ont., April 23, 1943.
Goaltender. Shoots left. 5'11", 185 lbs.
Last amateur club: Michigan Tech.

Season	Club	Lea	Regular Schedule				Playoffs			
			GP	GA	SO	GAPG	GP	GA	SO	GAPG
1967-68	Vancouver	WHL	62	199	4	3.20	--	--	--	--
1968-69	Mtl. Canadiens	NHL	12⅓	34	2	2.73	--	--	--	--
1968-69	Houston	CHL	19	46	1	2.42	1	3	0	3.00
1969-70	Chicago	NHL	63	136	15a	2.17	8	27	0	3.37
	NHL Totals		75⅓	170	17	2.26	8	27	0	3.37

a New NHL record for shutouts in regular season.

FERGUSON, JOHN BOWIE

Born, Vancouver, B.C., September 5, 1938.
Left wing. Shoots left. 5'11", 190 lbs.
Last amateur club: Fort Wayne Komets (Srs.).

Season	Club	Lea	Regular Schedule					Playoffs				
			GP	G	A	TP	PIM	GP	G	A	TP	PIM
1960-61	Cleveland	AHL	62	13	21	34	126	--	--	--	--	--
1961-62	Cleveland	AHL	70	20	21	41	146	6	2	2	4	6
1962-63	Cleveland	AHL	72	38	40	78	179	7	3	3	6	17
1963-64	Mtl. Canadiens	NHL	59	18	27	45	125	7	0	1	1	25
1964-65	Mtl. Canadiens	NHL	69	17	27	44	156	13	3	1	4	28
1966-67	Mtl. Canadiens	NHL	65	11	14	25	153	10	2	0	2	*44
1965-66	Mtl. Canadiens	NHL	67	20	22	42	*177	10	4	2	6	22
1967-68	Mtl. Canadiens	NHL	61	15	18	33	117	13	3	5	8	25
1968-69a	Mtl. Canadiens	NHL	71	29	23	52	185	14	4	3	7	*80
1969-70	Mtl. Canadiens	NHL	48	19	13	32	139					
	NHL Totals		440	129	144	273	1052	67	16	12	28	224

a NHL record for penalty minutes in one playoff-year.

HOWE, GORDON

Born, Floral, Sask., March 31, 1928.
Right wing. Shoots right. 6', 205 lbs.
Last amateur club: Saskatoon Lions Club Juveniles.

Season	Club	Lea	Regular Schedule					Playoffs				
			GP	G	A	TP	PIM	GP	G	A	TP	PIM
1945-46	Omaha	USHL	51	22	26	48	53	6	2	1	3	15
1946-47	Detroit	NHL	58	7	15	22	52	5	0	0	0	18
1947-48	Detroit	NHL	60	16	28	44	63	10	1	1	2	11
1948-49	Detroit	NHL	40	12	25	37	57	11	8	3	*11	19
1949-50	Detroit	NHL	70	35	33	68	69	1	0	0	0	7
1950-51a	Detroit	NHL	70	*43	*43	*86	74	6	4	3	7	4
1951-52ab	Detroit	NHL	70	*47	39	*86	78	8	2	*5	*7	2
1952-53ab	Detroit	NHL	70	*49	*46	*95	57	6	2	5	7	2
1953-54a	Detroit	NHL	70	33	*48	*81	109	12	4	5	9	*31
1954-55	Detroit	NHL	64	29	33	62	68	11	*9	11	*20	24
1955-56	Detroit	NHL	70	38	41	79	100	10	3	9	12	8
1956-57ab	Detroit	NHL	70	*44	45	*89	72	5	2	5	7	6
1957-58b	Detroit	NHL	64	33	44	77	40	4	1	1	2	0
1958-59	Detroit	NHL	70	32	46	78	57					
1959-60b	Detroit	NHL	70	28	45	73	46	6	1	5	6	4
1960-61	Detroit	NHL	64	23	49	72	30	11	4	11	*15	10
1961-62	Detroit	NHL	70	33	44	77	54					
1962-63ab	Detroit	NHL	70	*38	48	*86	100	11	7	9	*16	22
1963-64	Detroit	NHL	69	26	47	73	70	14	*9	10	*19	16
1964-65	Detroit	NHL	70	29	47	76	104	7	4	2	6	20
1965-66	Detroit	NHL	70	29	46	75	83	12	4	6	10	12
1966-67	Detroit	NHL	69	25	40	65	53	--	--	--	--	--
1967-68	Detroit	NHL	74	39	43	82	53	--	--	--	--	--
1968-69	Detroit	NHL	76	44	59	103	58	--	--	--	--	--
1969-70	Detroit	NHL	76	31	40	71	58	4	2	0	2	0
	NHL Totals		1624	763	994	1757	1605	154	67	91	158	216

a Art Ross Trophy.
b Hart Trophy.

HULL, ROBERT MARVIN (BOBBY)

Born, Point Anne, Ont., January 3, 1939
Left wing. Shoots left. 5'10", 193 lbs.
Last amateur club: St. Catharines (Jrs.).

			Regular Schedule					Playoffs				
Season	Club	Lea	GP	G	A	TP	PIM	GP	G	A	TP	PIM
1957-58	Chicago	NHL	70	13	34	47	62	--	--	--	--	--
1958-59	Chicago	NHL	70	18	32	50	50	6	1	1	2	2
1959-60a	Chicago	NHL	70	*39	42	*81	68	3	1	0	1	2
1960-61	Chicago	NHL	67	31	25	56	43	12	4	10	14	4
1961-62a	Chicago	NHL	70	*50	34	*84	35	12	*8	5	13	10
1962-63	Chicago	NHL	65	31	31	62	27	5	*8	2	10	4
1963-64	Chicago	NHL	70	*43	44	87	50	7	2	5	7	2
1964-65cd	Chicago	NHL	61	39	32	71	32	14	*10	7	*17	27
1965-66ade	Chicago	NHL	65	*54	43	*97	70	6	2	2	4	10
1966-67	Chicago	NHL	66	*52	28	80	52	6	4	2	6	0
1967-68	Chicago	NHL	71	*44	31	75	39	11	4	6	10	15
1968-69b	Chicago	NHL	74	*58	49	107	48	--	--	--	--	--
1969-70	Chicago	NHL	61	38	29	67	8	8	3	8	11	2
	NHL Totals	880	510	454	964	584	90	47	48	95	78

a Won Art Ross Trophy.
b NHL record for goals scored in regular season.
c Won Lady Byng Memorial Trophy.
d Won Hart Trophy.
e NHL record for points collected in regular season.

KEON, DAVID MICHAEL

Born, Normanda, Que., March 22, 1940.
Center. Shoots left. 5'9", 163 lbs.
Last amateur club: St. Michael's College (Jrs.).

			Regular Schedule					Playoffs				
Season	Club	Lea	GP	G	A	TP	PIM	GP	G	A	TP	PIM
1959-60	Sudbury	EPHL	--	--	--	--	--	4	2	2	4	2
1960-61a	Toronto	NHL	70	20	25	45	6	5	1	1	2	0
1961-62b	Toronto	NHL	64	26	35	61	2	12	5	3	8	0
1962-63b	Toronto	NHL	68	28	28	56	2	10	7	5	12	0
1963-64	Toronto	NHL	70	23	37	60	6	14	7	2	9	2
1964-65	Toronto	NHL	65	21	29	50	10	6	2	2	4	2
1965-66	Toronto	NHL	69	24	30	54	4	4	0	2	2	0
1966-67c	Toronto	NHL	66	19	33	52	2	12	3	5	8	0
1967-68	Toronto	NHL	67	11	37	48	4	--	--	--	--	--
1968-69	Toronto	NHL	75	27	34	61	12	4	1	3	4	2
1969-79	Toronto	NHL	72	32	30	62	6	--	--	--	--	--
	NHL Totals	686	231	318	549	54	67	26	23	49	6

a Won Calder Memorial Trophy.
b Won Lady Byng Memorial Trophy.
c Won Conn Smythe Trophy.

MAHOVLICH, FRANCIS WILLIAM (FRANK)

Born, Timmons, Ont., January 10, 1938.
Left wing. Shoots left. 6', 205 lbs.
Last amateur club: St. Michael's College (Jrs.).

Season	Club	Lea	GP	G	A	TP	PIM	GP	G	A	TP	PIM
1956-57	Toronto	NHL	3	1	0	1	2	--	--	--	--	--
1957-58a	Toronto	NHL	67	20	16	36	67	--	--	--	--	--
1958-59	Toronto	NHL	63	22	27	49	94	12	6	5	11	18
1959-60	Toronto	NHL	70	18	21	39	61	10	3	1	4	27
1960-61	Toronto	NHL	70	48	36	84	131	5	1	1	2	6
1961-62	Toronto	NHL	70	33	38	71	87	12	6	6	12	*29
1962-63	Toronto	NHL	67	36	37	73	56	9	0	2	2	8
1963-64	Toronto	NHL	70	26	29	55	66	14	4	*11	15	20
1964-65	Toronto	NHL	59	23	28	51	76	6	0	3	3	9
1965-66	Toronto	NHL	68	32	24	56	68	4	1	0	1	10
1966-67	Toronto	NHL	63	18	28	46	44	12	3	7	10	8
1967-68	Toronto	NHL	50	19	17	36	30	--	--	--	--	--
	Detroit	NHL	13	7	9	16	2	--	--	--	--	--
1968-69	Detroit	NHL	76	49	29	78	38	--	--	--	--	--
1969-70	Detroit	NHL	74	38	32	70	59	4	0	0	0	2
	NHL Totals		883	390	371	761	881	88	24	36	60	137

a Won Calder Memorial Trophy.

Traded to Detroit by Toronto with Garry Unger, Pete Stemkowski and rights to Carl Brewer in exchange for Paul Henderson, Norm Ullman and Floyd Smith, March 3, 1968.

MIKITA, STANLEY

Born, Sokolce, Czechoslovakia, May 20, 1940.
Center. Shoots right. 5'9", 165 lbs.
Last amateur club: St. Catharines (Jrs.).

Season	Club	Lea	GP	G	A	TP	PIM	GP	G	A	TP	PIM
1958-59	Chicago	NHL	3	0	1	1	4	--	--	--	--	--
1959-60	Chicago	NHL	67	8	18	26	119	3	0	1	1	2
1960-61	Chicago	NHL	66	19	34	53	100	12	*6	5	11	21
1961-62ab	Chicago	NHL	70	25	52	77	97	12	6	*15	*21	19
1962-63	Chicago	NHL	65	31	45	76	69	6	3	2	5	2
1963-64c	Chicago	NHL	70	39	50	*89	146	7	3	6	9	8
1964-65c	Chicago	NHL	70	28	*59	*87	154	14	3	7	10	*53
1965-66	Chicago	NHL	68	30	*48	78	58	6	1	2	3	2
1966-67cde	Chicago	NHL	70	35	*62	*97	12	6	2	2	4	2
1967-68cde	Chicago	NHL	72	40	47	*87	14	11	5	7	12	6
1968-69	Chicago	NHL	74	30	67	97	52	--	--	--	--	--
1969-70	Chicago	NHL	76	39	47	86	50	8	4	6	10	2
	NHL Totals		771	324	530	854	875	85	33	53	86	117

a NHL Stanley Cup Playoff Scoring Record.
b NHL Record for assists in Stanley Cup Playoffs.
c Art Ross Trophy.
d Hart Trophy.
e Lady Byng Trophy.

ORR, ROBERT GORDON (BOBBY)

Born, Parry Sound, Ont., March 20, 1948.
Defense. Shoots left. 5'11", 180 lbs.
Last amateur club: Oshawa, Ont. (Jrs.).

Season	Club	Lea	Regular Schedule					Playoffs				
			GP	G	A	TP	PIM	GP	G	A	TP	PIM
1966-67a	Boston	NHL	61	13	28	41	102	--	--	--	--	--
1967-68b	Boston	NHL	46	11	20	31	63	4	0	2	2	2
1968-69bc	Boston	NHL	67	21	43	64	133	10	1	7	8	10
1969-70cde	Boston	NHL	76	33	87	120	125	14	9	11	20	14
	NHL Totals		250	78	178	256	423	28	10	20	30	26

a Won Calder Memorial Trophy.
b Won James Norris Memorial Trophy.
c NHL record for goals in regular season by a defenseman.
d NHL record for assists in regular season by a defenseman.
e NHL record for total points in regular season by a defenseman.

PARK, DOUGLAS BRADFORD (BRAD)

Born, Toronto, Ont., July 6, 1948.
Defense. Shoots left. 6', 190 lbs.
Last amateur club: Toronto Marlboros (Jrs.).

Season	Club	Lea	Regular Schedule					Playoffs				
			GP	G	A	TP	PIM	GP	G	A	TP	PIM
1968-69	Buffalo	AHL	17	2	12	14	49	--	--	--	--	--
1968-69	NY Rangers	NHL	54	3	23	26	70	4	0	2	2	7
1969-70	NY Rangers	NHL	60	11	26	37	98	5	1	2	3	11
	NHL Totals		114	14	49	63	168	9	1	4	5	18

SANDERSON, DEREK MICHAEL

Born, Niagara Falls, Ont., June 16, 1946.
Center. Shoots left. 6', 176 lbs.
Last amateur club: Niagara Falls Flyers (Jrs.).

Season	Club	Lea	Regular Schedule					Playoffs				
			GP	G	A	TP	PIM	GP	G	A	TP	PIM
1965-66	Oklahoma City	CPHL	2	1	0	1	0	4	0	4	4	5
1965-66	Boston	NHL	2	0	0	0	0	--	--	--	--	--
1966-67	Boston	NHL	2	0	0	0	0	--	--	--	--	--
1966-67	Oklahoma City	CPHL						2	0	0	0	0
1967-68a	Boston	NHL	71	24	25	49	98	4	0	0	0	0
1968-69	Boston	NHL	61	26	22	48	146	9	*8	2	10	36
1969-70	Boston	NHL	50	18	23	41	118	14	5	4	9	72
		NHL Totals	186	68	70	138	362	27	13	8	21	117

a Won Calder Memorial Trophy.

SAVARD, SERGE

Born, Montreal, Que., January 22, 1946.
Defense. Shoots left. 6'2", 200 lbs.
Last amateur club: Junior Canadiens.

Season	Club	Lea	Regular Schedule					Playoffs				
			GP	G	A	TP	PIM	GP	G	A	TP	PIM
1964-65	Omaha	CPHL	2	0	0	0	0	4	0	1	1	4
1966-67	Mtl. Canadiens	NHL	2	0	0	0	0	--	--	--	--	--
1966-67	Quebec	AHL						1	0	0	0	2
1966-67a	Houston	CPHL	68	7	25	32	155	5	1	3	4	17
1967-68	Mtl. Canadiens	NHL	67	2	13	15	34	6	2	0	2	0
1968-69	Mtl. Canadiens	NHL	74	8	23	31	73	14	4	6	10	24
1969-70	Mtl. Canadiens	NHL	64	12	19	31	38	--	--	--	--	--
		NHL Totals	207	22	55	77	145	20	6	6	12	24

TKACZUK, WALTER ROBERT (WALT)

Born, Emstedetten, Germany, September 29, 1947.
Center. Shoots left. 6', 185 lbs.
Last amateur club: Kitchener Rangers (Jrs.).

Season	Club	Lea	GP	G	A	TP	PIM	GP	G	A	TP	PIM
			Regular Schedule					Playoffs				
1966-67	Omaha	CPHL	--	--	--	--	--	3	2	0	2	2
1967-68	NY Rangers	NHL	2	0	0	0	0	--	--	--	--	--
1968-69	Buffalo	AHL	5	2	7	9	9	--	--	--	--	--
1968-69	NY Rangers	NHL	71	12	24	36	28	4	0	1	1	6
1969-70	NY Rangers	NHL	76	27	50	77	38	6	2	1	3	17
		NHL Totals	149	39	74	113	66	10	2	2	4	23

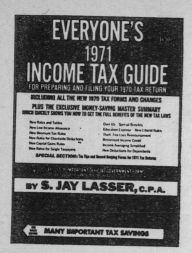

LATEST PYRAMID BESTSELLERS

DOSSIER IX, Barry Weil	N-2243/95¢
HOWARD HUGHES, John Keats	V-2220/$1.25
THE DANGEROUS MONTH OF MAY, Edward Henry Russell	N-2221/95¢
THE STRIKER PORTFOLIO, Adam Hall	N-2197/95¢
THE COEDS, Alison Lord	T-2160/75¢
AND TO MY NEPHEW ALBERT, David Forrest	T-2185/75¢
THE CROSS AND THE SWITCHBLADE, David Wilkerson	N-2189/95¢
LOVING, J. M. Ryan	N-2188/95¢
A KISS BEFORE DYING, Ira Levin	T-2158/75¢
SAM'S SONG, Shirley Schoonover	N-2140/95¢
THE PROMISE OF SPACE, Arthur C. Clarke	V-2157/$1.25

NOTE: PYRAMID pays postage on orders for 4 books or more. On orders for less than 4 books, add 10¢ per copy for postage and handling.

— — WHEREVER PAPERBACKS ARE SOLD OR USE THIS COUPON — — —

PYRAMID BOOKS
Dept. K234, 9 Garden Street, Moonachie, New Jersey 07074

Please send me the BESTSELLERS I have circled below. I enclose $_____

N2243	V2220	N2221	N2197	T2160	T2185
N2189	N2188	T2158	N2140	V2157	

NAME_____

ADDRESS_____

CITY_____STATE_____ZIP_____

I f you have enjoyed this book, you will want to read other inexpensive Pyramid best-sellers. You will find them wherever paperbacks are sold or you can order them direct from the pub-lisher. *Yours For The Asking:* a free, illustrated catalogue listing more than 700 books published by Pyramid. Write the publisher: PYRAMID BOOKS, Dept. K-99, 9 Garden Street, Moonachie, N. J. 07074.